THE BI

"Got 5 minutes while waiting for a phone call? Instead of checking email -- again -- take a bite of The Bite-Sized Entrepreneur. You'll find plenty of tips to stay motivated and productive, and build your business while building your life."
--Laura Vanderkam, author of Off The Clock: Feel Less Busy While Getting More Done

"In The Bite-Sized Entrepreneur, Damon Brown lays waste to both the misconceptions and pesky little lies we tell ourselves about why we can't make our side hustles a reality. A thoughtful, provocative read, Brown will help you understand why you have more time than you think to follow your passions—and offers smart, actionable advice to help you implement the right strategies so you can make your side hustle successful within the boundaries of the life you live today."
–Kayt Sukel, author of The Art of Risk and This Is Your Brain On Sex

"*In* The Ultimate Bite-Sized Entrepreneur, *Damon Brown proves that you don't need to don a hoodie, move to Silicon Valley and sacrifice all your sleep (and sanity) to make it in the world of self-employment. Through his road-tested wisdom and interviews with successful innovators who have built businesses on their own terms, Damon provides practical, tactical advice to grow your business one small, delicious, perfectly bite-sized step at a time.*"
--Jenny Blake, *author of Pivot: The Only Move That Matters Is Your Next One*

"*You can create the life you imagined and still be an entrepreneur. Damon's new book will give you the easy way to implement strategies and do just that. Entrepreneurship is the best gig ever* only *if you do it the way Damon lays out. Otherwise, you'll be working for the worst boss you ever had.*"
--Cameron Herold, *author of* Double Double: How to Double Your Revenue and Profit in 3 Years or Less

"For every would-be entrepreneur who's wondered if it's possible to "crush it" without crushing yourself, this book is for you! In this concise read, Inc. columnist Damon Brown lays out a road map for launching a satisfying and successful business without overturning the life you currently have."
–Meagan Francis, founder, the Life, Listened podcast network

"Sure, it starts with passion, but what do you know about living the life of an entrepreneur? The Bite-Sized Entrepreneur gives smart, succinct advice about how to follow your business dreams, including why to treat Tuesday like Monday; the difference between busyness and productivity; and three effective ways of saying 'no.' Highly recommended for would-be entrepreneurs and freelancers."

--Kelly K. James, author of Six-Figure Freelancing, Second Edition: The Writer's Guide to Make More Money

THE ULTIMATE BITE-SIZED ENTREPRENEUR TRILOGY

BITE-SIZED ENTREPRENEUR BOOK #4
76 WAYS TO BOOST
TIME, PRODUCTIVITY & FOCUS ON
YOUR BIG IDEA

Damon Brown
Inc.com columnist &
Co-Founder of Cuddlr
www.JoinDamon.me

TWITTER/INSTAGRAM: *@BROWNDAMON*
CONSULTING & SPEAKING REQUESTS:
DAMON@DAMONBROWN.NET

PUBLISHED BY:
Damon Brown

The Ultimate Bite-Sized Entrepreneur Trilogy
1st Edition
2018 Revision
Copyright 2017 by Damon Brown
Edited by Jeanette Hurt
Cover designed by Bec Loss

This book includes the first three books in the Bite-Sized Entrepreneur trilogy as well as additional writing. Some material has been graciously reprinted or inspired by my work on Inc. Magazine Online, within random tweets, and on scribbled index cards. Thank you.

To Bernadette Johnson.
Thank you for clearing a path, Ma.

Lindsay!

Keep up the entrepreneurship!

All my best,

Silvana LeBog
'18

"What is the work that you can't not do?"

-Scott Dinsmore,
How to find work you love

Reading

ON BALANCE

(FROM THE BALANCED BITE-SIZED ENTREPRENEUR)

MORE FUEL

FOREWORD

I wrote THE BITE-SIZED ENTREPRENEUR book to understand how things manifested so quickly. Three years before writing it, I was a San Franciscan tech journalist seriously dating a wonderful woman. Less than a thousand days later, I was a married San Diegan in a house with a white picket fence (Seriously!), taking care of my 1-year-old son and reeling from the sale of my first startup, Cuddlr. How did I transform so quickly? Like Aurelius' *Meditations* or David Thoreau's *Walden*, this book was an elaborate note to self.

What remains humbling is that you have experienced the same question: How can I fulfill my calling while keeping my life intact? I'm honored to be on this journey with you, and this special edition captures the best of THE BITE-SIZED ENTREPRENEUR trilogy along with exclusive discussions directly influenced by meeting people like you at during my talks all around the world.

Whenever I am in need, I love to pull my favorite philosophical book off the shelf, pick a random page, and take in the wisdom. It always seems to be what I need to hear at the time. My intention, and my hope, is for this ultimate collection to play the same role in your life.

-Damon Brown, November 2017

ON STARTING (THE BITE-SIZED ENTREPRENEUR)

To Alec,
who inspired me to do my first TED Talk &
build my first successful startup before he could
even speak.
Thank you.

"Most of us have two lives. The life we live, and the unlived life within us. Between the two stands Resistance"

-Steven Pressfield, The War of Art

A WORD ON PASSION

Passion is the compass that points you in the right direction above the fog of the moment and the uncertainty of the future. Passion is also the instinct that pushes you to destroy everything else to get that brass ring.

Passion will leave you stranded if you do not put in the time. Passion will also give you the heart of steel needed to thrive when the less dedicated will falter.

Passion is our vice and our victory. Use it wisely.

Introducing You,
the Bite-Sized Entrepreneur

I never intended to be an entrepreneur. I just had an idea.

At the time, I was a freelance tech journalist living in San Francisco. A friend of mine was struggling to remember a quote. I asked, innocently, "Isn't there an app for that?" There wasn't, and I found myself becoming an entrepreneur for the same reason most creators do: I realized something I needed did not exist and, if I didn't create it, it might never exist.

The odd part wasn't the journey to creating what would become the app So Quotable: it was who was actually making the journey. I wasn't a young, hooded Harvard dropout like Facebook's Zuckerberg, nor was I a brash, brilliant college dropout like Apple's Jobs, nor a rich, hip L. A. kid like Snapchat's Spiegel.

I was a journalist and author, an African American man in his mid-30s who, aside from negotiating rates with magazines, had no business experience.

In fact, at the time, I was about to propose to my now-wife. By the time So Quotable ramped up to launch three years later, I had bought my first home, married that long-time girlfriend, and we had our first kid. In the midst of the launch, a colleague helping out on the tech side bailed, and I found myself learning Apple's iPhone programming language with one hand while rocking my newborn in my other, spare arm.

I wasn't sure if the app – or even I – would make it to the finish line, but I also had not felt so alive in a long time. I'd wake up in the middle of the night with new ideas and realize elegant solutions to my app challenges during dinnertime. It was like I had two babies instead of just one. It was the passion to make my mark: I wasn't staying up late and getting up ridiculously early to watch my favorite show or to have "me" time. It was a nobler cause.

I was also doing things my way. Instead of staying in Silicon Valley, ditching my girlfriend, and dressing like a college student, I moved out of Silicon Valley, settled down behind my proverbial white picket fence, and created the type of entrepreneurial life that I envisioned.

And, to my surprise, it worked. So Quotable launched in time for my first TED talk and gained a great cult following. The success connected me with two others to launched Cuddlr, a social plutonic app for connecting for hugs. Cuddlr hit #1 on the Apple App store twice, got us on the cover of *The Wall Street Journal*, and was acquired less than a year after it arrived. I handled the Cuddlr launch through daily 4 a.m. Skype calls with my international colleagues, with occasional breaks to coax my new toddler back to sleep.

The truth is that the success didn't happen with the media coverage, the TED talk, or even the Cuddlr acquisition, but from doing and completing the work. As they say in Silicon Valley, real creators ship – and the product shipped! As soon as I met someone, told them about So Quotable, and said "You can download it off the Apple App Store now," I won.

You absolutely have the ability to follow your passion, fulfill a public or personal need, and make a legacy for yourself within the structure of your 9-to-5, your family life, or your daily grind. Never before have we been more capable to pursue our passions within the time we have. Like kids jumping Double Dutch rope, we have more room for our dreams than we think – it's just a matter of good strategy and timing. And perhaps that side hustle we create will become the foundation for the rest of our careers.

Bite-sized entrepreneurs incorporate brilliant startup techniques into their daily lives, giving themselves the focus and drive to pursue new passions while still being true to where they are in their personal and professional lives. *The belief that you have to sacrifice your livelihood to leave your entrepreneurial mark is a lie.* It isn't about losing the life you have, but adding value to create the life you want.

There are many things a bite-sized entrepreneur is not. She is not a dilettante, dabbling in various pursuits to combat boredom or gain prestige; a bite-sized entrepreneur doesn't give up when things get difficult. She is not a shallow businessperson, keeping the dedication superficial; a bite-sized entrepreneur dedicates every available ounce of free time to understanding her passion. She is not an obligated creator, getting her ego too invested into the idea to change; a bite-sized entrepreneur gives her passion space to transform organically into the business it was meant to be. Finally, she is not a patient person, assuming that one day she'll have all the time in the world to pursue her true passion; a bite-sized entrepreneur ain't waiting until retirement.

I'd love to be your guide on your entrepreneurial journey. Like my *Inc. Magazine* online column which inspired this book, I am giving you simple, digestible, and actionable insights that can be interwoven into your current life structure. You can flip through the 21 strategies in any order, though you may notice a natural flow if you read it straight from top to bottom. All of these ideas are explored with people who have successfully executed what you currently feel: A calling to create something bigger than yourself within the parameters of your current life. Everyone's journey is different, which is the point: Realizing your business aspirations is not, and should not, be a one-size-fits-all process. Let's make an impact on our own terms. Today.

-Damon Brown, August 2016

"Rule of thumb: The more important a call or action to our soul's evolution, the more Resistance we will feel towards pursuing it."

-Steven Pressfield, The War of Art

1

THE PASSION TRAP
Passion favors sweaty palms

Are you waiting for inspiration? Passion? A muse? I wouldn't count on it. When it comes to business, particularly entrepreneurship, you're better off leaning on just doing the work.

Artist and entrepreneur Jessica Abel describes the process well:

Passion for a practice or a subject comes from your investment of time and energy. Whatever your passion turns out to be is a combination of what you're into, your circumstances, and what happens to fall across your path, added to what you decide to spend your time on and what you're willing to take risks to do more of, with a just a tiny dash of natural talent.

The term "practice" has a double meaning. We have you practicing something every day, like playing the piano. We also have you doing the practice, as in growing the mental and emotional discipline to stay committed to a goal. It's not a coincidence that the same word is used in daily rituals and commitments, like meditation.

The truth is that passion will not get you out of bed every morning. Like love, it can be fickle and moody and fairweather. Passion makes you more susceptible to burnout and extreme thinking.

Doing the work, though? It sustains you, because it never changes, and it gives levity when things are great and when things suck.

All you have to do is show up every day.

2
LIES WE TELL
Be gentle with others, give yourself tough love

We all share common challenges when it comes to the tough road of entrepreneurship, but we also give common comforts to ourselves to push into another day.

In short, we lie to ourselves.

You don't know if the rockstar client will come through, a successful fundraise will happen or even if a larger competitor will snuff you out. There has to be a suspension of disbelief--otherwise, you wouldn't attempt to run your own business in the first place. Passion sometimes needs a little help trumping common sense.

There's absolutely nothing wrong with having faith in the future, but it is crucial that we recognize the times when we're placating ourselves for self-management. Here are the biggest comforts I say to myself. Perhaps you can relate.

I'll start this project/this business when I have more bandwidth
There is always tomorrow--until there is not. Like becoming a parent, there will never be an ideal

time to launch your business. You will always need more resources than you have, more time than you got, and more energy than you can muster. If Steve Jobs, Elon Musk, and other visionaries waited until everything was perfect, then we wouldn't be talking about Jobs, Musk and their contemporaries right now.

As wine seller turned successful entrepreneur Gary Vaynerchuk said in an impassioned message: "I worked weekends and holidays every day starting at fourteen years old to make [my business] happen. I think back to all the time I put in of real, hard work before I saw any of the benefits." Don't wait for a red carpet.

I'll save my business/my finances if I can just net this one client
One client often isn't enough to save your business. Worse, if you put all your focus on netting one client, all things tend to fall to the wayside (even if you do get the client).

For instance, if your company gets any acquisition or investment interest, it is easy to start focusing on the potential payoff rather than the day-to-day work and the long-term strategy. And if it falls through, your company will take a while to get back on course--assuming it ever will.

I'll stay up all night/skip today's meals because that's how you crush it

Entrepreneurs will have you believe that skipping that night of sleep or "crushing it" all day without eating is the key to success--there is even a startup or two dedicated to the idea. Sacrifices need to be made (I definitely walk the walk on that one), but there is no real correlation between depriving your body of needs and creating the next unicorn startup. In fact, you are more likely to burn out. Pushing yourself beyond your limits should be viewed as a contextually necessary evil, not as a default.

Consider this: If you do successfully reach that fundraising/monetization/users goal, then you'll have another goal after that and a business that will demand even more from you. I know many an entrepreneur who flamed out before reaching even the first milestone, defeating the whole purpose of moving forward. We often work harder than we should because we want to feel like we're crushing it--and that feel is more important than the actual impact. There is a difference between killing it and killing yourself.

I'll get work done on the plane/vacation/break

There is always more work to do: Another email to send, another pitch to perfect, and another glitch to correct. A major challenge is allowing ourselves to get away. The second part of the challenge? Letting others allow us to get away.

We assume we'll get work done on the flight in or during our travels, so we start pushing work into that so-called free time and start making promises that we may not be able to keep. It usually has one of two outcomes: You actually begin to relax after you realize how exhausted you are, but carry the guilt of making promises you won't keep, or you stress yourself out juggling the demands of travel and the needs of work, not really resting and, likely, not doing your best work because you are tired. Sometimes when you try to do two things, you actually fail at both.

I'll work with this PITA client one last time

Stop lying to yourself. Money, sympathy, or even status quo can compel us to repeat a client who is a pain in the ass (PITA). When we get another opportunity to work with the client, we tend to forget about the issues that stressed us out in the first place--like parents deciding to have another kid. It's not until you're knee-deep in the same situation that you say, "Ah, that's why I swore I'd never work with them again."

Assume that you'll get another, better client (or clients) to replace them. Our fear is often driven by the feast or famine cycle: Keep every client you have, as you don't know when you'll get another one! In reality, we can't actually get new, quality clients if we're spending all our time inefficiently catering to our ill-fitting ones.

I need to quit my job/end my relationships so I can truly dedicate myself to my big idea
Kids will come, money will go, and jobs are necessary, but time is the one asset you can't get back. Waiting for a big chunk of time is usually a waste of time. You fall into the extreme thinking trap: You need to go big or not go at all. There are certain times when you have to leap, but that's usually after you've already recognized an opportunity and have done the homework... and that work takes time.

Keep in mind that Twitter, Yammer, and other billion dollar companies began as side projects founders did while focusing on their day job. Imagine if they waited until they could "go big". Plant the seed today.

3

EFFECTIVE PROCRASTINATION
What you aren't procrastinating on is more important

Procrastination is a bad, four-letter word, something to be avoided at all costs. For entrepreneurs, it is a sin somewhere between working for free and being a poor networker. I recently heard a quote, though, that changed my outlook on procrastination:

"The work you do while you procrastinate is the work you should do for the rest of your life." - Jessica Hische

Procrastination is usually viewed as the absence of work (and, therefore, the loss of profit and productivity), but what if it was a compass to your true calling? Perhaps the things you do that make time fly by faster can be integrated into your actual work.

In retrospect, the procrastination idea has already changed my career. I was perfectly happy researching and writing books, but writing my first major book, *Porn & Pong: How Grand Theft Auto, Tomb Raider and Other Sexy Games Changed Our Culture*, on the history of sexuality and video games, put me on my first book tour. It was amazing! I spent five years working in solitude, and now I was finally able to discuss my theories and share my inside stories with the world. In fact, I began to enjoy the in-person intimacy more than the actual writing. I could have ignored that impulse and gone back to writing, but instead I shifted my focus to public speaking and soon got onto the TED stage doing more of what I love.

I would delay getting back to my writing so I could connect with people. Now I craft dynamic speeches in addition to writing books, turning my procrastination vice into my strength - and integrating my previous career into it in the process.

Here's how you can turn your procrastination into a powerful tool:

Listen
What activity are you doing now to prevent you from going back to the work you claim to enjoy? Mindless activities, or what you do without feeling stressed, could represent you going on instinct rather than forced action. In other words, figure out what you do in your life that feels natural.

Distill
What are the basic traits of your procrastination? Write down what you actually get from the activity. My love of long conversations boils down to connecting with others, getting different

viewpoints, and arguing new ideas. Think about your own favorite procrastination and distill it down to two or three things you get out of it - without judgment.

Pivot

How can you integrate your natural inclinations into your practice? For instance, if you love sitting in a coffee shop talking for hours, then perhaps you need more face time with your clients. It doesn't mean you have to change your entire business, but that you are pivoting to include more of what you actually love.

How can you integrate your favorite procrastination into your business life?

4
IDEA DEBT
Too many ideas mean none get done

I recently did an idea purge. I love committing my thoughts down onto index cards since they are simple, portable, and easy to organize. I started decluttering over recent months and I realized my pile of cards has gotten out of hand. The most amazing discovery: A new idea I thought I came up with was written on a piece of paper from a year before! Talk about going in circles.

If I could have smacked myself in my own head, I would have.

Author Kazu Kibuishi has a great term for this psychological weight: **Idea debt**.

I try not to look at what I'm going to do as this amazing great grand thing. I'm not just fulfilling some old promise that I made a long time ago. Now I'm actually solving problems in the moment, and that's so much more exciting than trying to fill years of what I like to call my "idea debt." That's when you have this dream of this awesome thing for years. You think, "Oh, I'm going to do this epic adventure. It's going to be so great." The truth is, no matter what you do, it will never be as great as it is in your mind, and so you're really setting yourself up for failure.

Kibuishi is talking about perfectionism: Waiting for the perfect time to start the perfect idea. Entrepreneurs (and, in a tip to my background, journalists) can't have this perfectionist approach because we A) have to bow to bigger deadlines, and B) we would never survive as entrepreneurs. Point me to a founder who believes her product is perfect to ship and I'll show you someone who won't be a founder for long. There are always more ways to improve a product or service. Getting to market is the only reason why we should stop.

If perfectionism isn't the big problem for entrepreneurs, then what is the issue? Idealism. Underlying Kibuishi's description is the idealization, the grand structure, the bells and whistles of our great scheme. And the idealization, structure and bells and whistles of another great scheme. Oh, and the other one we have, too. As entrepreneurs, we often have too many things planned out that weigh on our daily lives. At least for me, the "cool ideas" I have are far outweighing the time, energy and, frankly, quality control I'm able to muster.

So, ideas are getting killed. Slaughtered. Put out to pasture. Index cards have been chucked, unfinished manuscripts have been tossed, and untouched research has been recycled.

I ask three questions with every jotted note:

Why haven't I executed on it yet?
Again, I found ideas from a decade ago. From my passionate productivity to my sacrifice of sleep, I've managed to pursue and complete many goals. Chances are, there is a legitimate reason why this idea is on an old scrap of paper versus being a properly executed plan.

Why am I holding on to it?
Often, the idea of something is way more powerful than the will to create it. And if it is that powerful of an idea, then it will come back stronger after you dump it.

Why am I defending it?
By keeping that idea lingering you have to, by nature, defend it against criticism from others and even from yourself - otherwise, the idea would have been forgotten long ago. Unfortunately, we are so encouraged to defend our ideas and our beliefs, it's easy to neglect that we've outgrown them. And those ideas take space from potential new projects.

As I've purged my unfinished, incomplete ideas, I've realized how much ego I have tied up into what *could* be.

What idea should you be letting go?

5

BUSYNESS
Be productive, not busy

Projects, people, and passions can keep us on the move, but there is a distinct difference between busyness and productivity. Productivity feels like you do not want to stop. Busyness feels like you cannot stop.

Chronic busyness is rampant today, even though we know that it isn't good for us. Why do we keep ourselves excessively busy? There are three big rewards we get out of it:

Fulfills the ego
Like sociologist Brene Brown's take on comparative suffering, our busyness has become an acute measurement of our entrepreneurial worth: "You stayed up all night? I've been up for 72 hours straight working on my business." What we tend not to brag about is efficiency, as the wiser person may have paused, strategized, and executed the same goal in a shorter period of time. It is definitely the age of the hustle, but I'd love to see us upgrade to the thoughtful hustle: How can we maximize our time? Busyness for the sake of busyness isn't it.

Fulfills the guilt
Feeling guilty when we actually do take a break is

common, particularly during crucial periods. Even notable entrepreneur Elon Musk famously said he is afraid of vacations. However, it is during the pivotal points in your business where you actually need to pace yourself to stave burnout. You can minimize your guilt by having a structure in place that actually allows your business to continue uninterrupted while you are away.

Fulfills the silence

Being still often scares us, as it can make us feel anxiously bored and even to think about the things we've been avoiding with busyness. There is so much to be discovered when we allow ourselves to stop and quiet down. In fact, we may suddenly be given an elegant answer to the challenge we've been so busy trying to conquer.

6
A GOOD BURNOUT
Always maximize your time on the sidelines

If there is one thing we don't talk about in entrepreneurship, it is burnout. Company failure, spousal abuse and self-destroying habits are often accepted, but you're not allowed to admit you are exhausted. I know people who were so burnt out that they just disappeared without a trace. No judgment from me: I walked the precarious line myself, juggling raising my baby, bootstrapping a top Apple app, and maintaining my writing career.

No one is Superman or Wonder Woman. It's a shame that we don't talk about burnout more because, like the proverbial dark night of the soul, there are some amazing, priceless gems we can gain only in the space between ending and doing. Keep these strategies in mind, particularly if you can actually make time to process your burnout.

Stop
Burnout means you don't have the energy or focus to continue on. It means excessive late nights, drawn-out meetings, and extra drama have to go away, simply because you physically, mentally, and emotionally can't carry the weight. Good! They shouldn't have been there in the first place.

In my reflective time after my startup was acquired, I've done judicious editing in my life: removing excess, ending relationships, and pausing action. Decisions are now based on gut, even if that means missing opportunities. Urgency is as addictive as envy, and just as deadly, since it is the comparison to the person you think you deserve to be as opposed to the comparison to the competitor you think you see. A forced pause makes you reconsider where you put your energy, since your stamina is now limited.

Restrategize

What are you actually working toward? The day-to-day grind leaves little to no room for actual strategy, as you've got real, tangible business problems at your doorstep. The problem is that you don't restrategize until you or a loved one gets sick, your career takes a left turn or... you suffer burnout. Burning out shouldn't be looked at as a failure, but as an internal switch going off to tell you the parts of your life that have been neglected need to be attended to. It might feel like the timing couldn't be worse, but it is always the right time for your body, mind, and soul.

The only way forward is to make career decisions more conducive to the life you need. As Warren Buffett famously said, the most valuable thing entrepreneurs can say is "No." What stuff are you carrying that you shouldn't have been carrying in the first place?

Prioritize

Like when I was guiding the growth of my startup, my time is limited to what must be done *now*. However, unlike an overflowing email box or an app update demanding my attention, the things that are demanding my time are my sons, my intuitive leaps toward new ideas, and my own personal balance. I'm still running on a compressed time schedule, except it isn't filled with work, but with self-care. In a sense, I'm still taking in the last startup roller coaster ride -- at least emotionally. And I'm already gaining more clarity on my higher purpose as an entrepreneur.

Whether your hamster wheel is a startup or a corporate gig, we all struggle to prioritize. Instead, we triage based on the values we had before we got on the ride -- prioritizing based on an outdated model that doesn't take into account anything we've learned before. Been doing the same thing for five years without a break? Then you are organizing and prioritizing your work, and your career, based on whatever you learned a half decade ago. It is difficult to take everything in while you're trying to put out the next fire, but it's not impossible.

Burnt out? Embrace it as much as you can. The next journey will begin soon enough.

7

CLUTTER

New opportunities can't come in without space

My office is filled with lots of mindfulness and strategic tools, but the most useful one is a brand-new shredder. It cost $50 with coupons. Powerful enough to eat through papers, folders, and credit cards for 30 minutes straight, the little monster turned my save-for-a-rainy-day piles into buckets of confetti. The debris filled two garbage cans roughly my height and width.

What are you still carrying that you don't need? The cathartic act of destruction, of removal, and of closure gives us space for our next act. It forces us to make peace with the past. It also gives us pause to honor what we've done.

The physical clutter

In one pile, for instance, I found my business card from a few years ago. It said JOURNALIST in big letters, proudly referred to publications that don't exist anymore, and highlighted projects and books that, at the time, represented the peak of my career. Speaking at TED was still a dream. Being a startup founder wasn't even on the radar. This random scrap piece of paper represented an acknowledgement of my growth, something that we entrepreneurs are want to do. It also made me realize that I was just as likely to find my 2016 business card one day and quietly acknowledge, again, how much my career had evolved–an inspiring, high-level thought while I do the day-to-day entrepreneurial march.

The virtual clutter

It can be just as inspiring to do a virtual purge. In fact, the real challenge in the future won't be us drowning in papers, but being overwhelmed by stuffed email accounts, bursting app screens, and bloated cloud drives. As I argued in *Our Virtual Shadow: Why We Are Obsessed with Documenting Our Lives Online*, "The way we are using technology, our idea is that we document everything now and sort it out later." Well, the sooner you make "later" happen, the more mental and emotional space you'll give for future growth.

It's overwhelming, but here is where you can start:
- **Buy a shredder or another efficiency-focused product.** It's worth getting services and products that will create room for your future business. The virtual side is equally important. For example, a computer efficiency program can delete orphaned data and compress your useful files so you can work faster.
- **Take an afternoon to assess.** Imagine you are working in a new office on a new computer.

We have unparalleled focus, clarity, and relief when we're working with a clean slate. Decluttering and deleting isn't on the same level, but spending three hours organizing can bring us much closer to that nirvana. Time is our most valuable asset, but the return on investment here is high.

- **Prevent indecisiveness by hiding your stuff.** If you are on the fence about tossing any physical or digital goods, try putting them away, like in a dark part of the closet or in a file deep within your computer memory. Check in a few months later. If you haven't accessed them, then you probably don't need them. The hiding technique is popular among clothing decluttering experts.

Sorting, removing, and tossing our entrepreneurial baggage may the ultimate way to assess our past—giving us clarity for which previous pitfalls to avoid and where we should be focusing on next.

When is the last time you cleared the decks?

"During the process of rising, we sometimes find ourselves homesick for a place that no longer exists. We want to go back to that moment, before we walked into the arena, but there's nowhere to go back to."

-Brene Brown, Rising Strong

8
GROWTH SPURT
Take extra care during any transitions

I am in a growth spurt, just like my toddler. My favorite entrepreneurial clothes, which fit perfectly yesterday, are ridiculously small today. Ideas are moving faster than my attention span can handle. I need more rest, yet I'm overstimulated by all the possibilities now. I've outgrown my past and am stretching hard to build my future. "Comfortable" is a word I haven't used in a very, very long time.

You could argue that entrepreneurs are always in a growth spurt, but that's not really true. You cannot always be expanding, changing and breaking your foundation, and as much as our ego wants us to believe we're always pushing boundaries, it isn't possible to be in a continual state of growth. In fact, not pausing to evaluate can actually hurt our progress. No, a growth spurt is when you are expanding your customer base to a new demographic, you are pivoting your company to a new arena or you are moving your business to another level. It is scary, frustrating and exhilarating.

I see it every day when I am with my toddler, just as I see it every day when I look at myself in the mirror. Here's how I take care of both of us:

Feed yourself well

You don't know what you're doing anymore, so everything takes more time and energy than planned. Let's face it: There is a certain amount of autopilot that happens when we have a good rhythm going. Now, that rhythm is gone.

Like a growing child, your appetite is absolutely insatiable. In the past six months since selling my startup, I have read more books, been more thoughtful and asked more questions than any other time in recent memory. Why? I'm spending every moment figuring out how the hell to structure this next phase. My brain needs to be fed.

Give space

Similar to my son, you need an unusual amount of space to grow. Unlike him, however, you already have responsibilities, obligations and patterns that can keep you from growing into better opportunities. For you, me and other adults, we gain space by saying No. A lot. (Actually, that's not too different from a toddler, either.)

It wasn't until well after I transformed from journalist to entrepreneur that I realized how much I needed to remove from my life: From restructuring my relationships to chucking out outdated ideas. To flip Shonda Rhimes' TED Talk celebrating her year of saying yes, creating a Year of No is one of the best things you can do for your business.

Follow desire

What risks did you want to take now that you were too afraid or unable to take before? The beautiful part about instability is that one smart, calculated risk could be as disruptive as two or three calculated risk - no matter how many changes you make, you know you will never be the previous person again. The past is gone and cannot be rewound. The previous rules don't apply anymore.

Passion is your only clear compass.

9

FAVORS THE PREPARED
Make a contingency plan for success

How do you prepare for failure? It makes sense to have a Plan B, like a nest egg you can crack if it all goes south, or a set vocation that you know is in demand, or perhaps an alternative business you can launch. Only the most risk-tolerent - and, perhaps, reckless - of us go into an endeavor without any type of security. In fact, it may be more motivation for you.

Now, how do you prepare for success? I've found that most of us have made peace with failing, but actually don't have a plan for when we succeed.
In 2014, I co-founded the social meetup app Cuddlr with a couple other people - super small operation with barely a budget. I spearheaded the launch strategy and mapped out our plan from pre-launch to about six months out. My co-founders expected a cult following, I expected a more mainstream opportunity. What we got was a smash hit, getting an incredible amount of press and running to the top of the Apple App store within its first week. We're lucky we had a framework plan for post-launch, but it was difficult to ride the rocket ship even with that. Imagine if we had no plan for success! We probably wouldn't have been acquired.

The challenge for my co-founders and me, as well as many entrepreneurs, was that our focus was on evangelizing our service. But what if people love our service? It becomes preaching to the choir. There has to be a strategy if you actually win. It's akin to a presidential candidate being focused on the debates, but not having a set plan for when she actually gets into office. It's a recipe for disaster - even though you got what you wanted.

Here is some food for thought.

Plan it all the way through
What if you get that gold-star client or make that financial goal this year? Consider the next goal you have in mind. For instance, what kind of maintenance will be required to keep that hard-to-get client? Or how, exactly, will you be using that additional profit from a financial milestone?

Line up your mentors
A fresh success often means dealing with new issues that require a brand new strategy. Do you have a brain trust ready? The key isn't to have people who know what you know, but know what you'll need to know once you succeed. Again, planning for success means you assume you'll need a higher level of insight.

Look at different types of success
Entrepreneurs like myself often have many

opportunities happening all at different stages, which means you may reach your goal with two medium-sized clients versus the big whale you've been trying to score. Does that affect the outcome? Run through a few ways success could happen for you. You may be surprised at how a slightly different outcome will affect your post-success strategy.

10
GOING PUBLIC
Recognition does not equal success

I'll never forget when my journalism law professor, the late Richard Schwarzlose, recommended I get E. B. White's *The New Journalism*. I was halfway through Northwestern's prestigious Magazine Publishing graduate program and realized that I didn't want to publish magazines. I wanted to write. "Go find *The New Journalism*" he said with a pat. "And you'll see what's possible." Published in 1973, *The New Journalism* had excerpts from edgy non-fiction writers who incorporated fiction techniques to unparalled effect. Tom Wolfe, Joan Didion, and Gay Talese were among them and are still considered literary giants today. I slept with the book under my pillow.

The most outrageous contributor was Hunter S. Thompson, the scoundrel who got in deep with The Hell's Angels, revealed southern racism at the Kentucky Derby, and truly exposed the dark side of Las Vegas. He consistently reported while being drunk and high and anti-social. He also was a master of words. To the untrained eye, it would be easy to assume that the former somehow enabled the latter. That would be a lie.

When Hunter S. Thompson died of an apparent

suicide in 2005, one of his most shared quotes was from an old 1974 *Playboy Magazine* interview:

"One day you just don't appear at the El Adobe bar anymore: You shut the door, paint the windows black, rent an electric typewriter and become the monster you always were – the writer."

In other words, behind Thompson's drunken binges and crazy partying was sober work. It is always work. It will always be work. Work is behind everything.

Today, it isn't necessarily cocaine sniffs and tequila chasers. It is tweeting about the next novel you are going to do when you haven't written the last five books you've talked about. It is launching a kickstarter campaign for something you know you don't have the passion to follow through on. It is networking at conferences, at parties, and at coffeeshops about your brilliant idea that you could have – should have – started literally years ago. It is the flash before the fire, the dessert before the main course.

It is cheating.

We worry about selling out for security or big bucks, but the most dangerous selling out is you removing the work and soaking in the fun and the accolades that are supposed to be a reward for that very work. There is mounting scientific proof that saying you are going to do something and getting props for it taps the same part of your brain that recognizes reward for actually *doing* it. In other words, you could lose the motivation to achieve your goal simply because you've already gotten part of the reward: Recognition.

The results are sad. It is the drunk journalist who doesn't know what questions to ask, it is the potential writer posting endlessly about the new book he should be drafting, and it is the wannabe entrepreneur publicizing an app that they haven't even started developing. What they fail to understand is that the real spoils aren't recognition, awards, or money, but growth, insight, and impact – and that only comes with work.

There is no hack to that.

11
DIRTY WORK
Get your hands dirty as much as possible

My best entrepreneurial moments happened when I was tasked something I had no business doing. In creating my first app, So Quotable, I spent the first few years getting lots of support from a tech-savvy friend. One random day before it was going to launch, this person disappeared without a trace – and with the code. I was pissed. So, while taking care of my newborn baby, I learned to program for Apple devices, designed the user interface, and released the app within four months. It came out in time for my first TED Talk.

As my co-founders and I launched my second app, Cuddlr, circumstances shifted my role from a silent media and cultural strategist to the public face of the app. By the time we were acquired a year later, I was doing the majority of the interviews.

I'm proud of how I rose to those occasions, but I share this because I am 100 percent, absolutely positive that I wouldn't have done any of this unless it was necessary. Who in their right mind would get up before dawn to program with one hand while rocking their infant in the other? No one, that's who.

When I talked to my best friend, author A. Raymond Johnson, about the So Quotable experience, I compared it to being a lounge singer that suddenly became a singer-songwriter. I always had a vision, but now I could see the concept, map it out, and release it my damn self. I was a one-man band. I was free. My experience with Cuddlr essentially doubled down on that feeling, as I led our tiny company through intense media blitzes, demanding customers, and an eventual acquisition. They were journeys that few entrepreneurs are able to experience from inside the arena.

You may not be able to afford a capable programmer, a strong PR team, or a great logo artist. It may be late nights of you proverbially mopping the floor, taking out the trash, and doing the dishes by hand. But when you eventually are able to hire others to help, you'll have an unmistakably keen vision for how to run your business efficiently and wisely.

It is an insight the suckers who simply hired out the dirty work will never, ever have.

12

SKIP MONDAY
Strategize early to better execute later

It usually happens around Sunday afternoon: The vague, uncomfortable reminder that tomorrow is Monday. You get revved up to start the week at your A-game, but the pressure can often crush any real or perceived progress. It can be a rough cycle.

Instead, consider shifting your usual Monday work to Tuesday. Whether your business is based on the traditional work week or loosely framed around consultant hours, it is a simple strategy that can save you both time and anxiety.

No one is paying attention on Monday
When do brands announce things they don't want to get attention? Friday afternoon. And despite the norm, I'd argue that Monday morning would be a close second, as everyone is antsy to get out what they've been working on or thinking about since late last week. The same can be said for important internal and external meetings, major sales launches and anything else that requires serious attention. It's like we all have a gag order for two and a half days and, suddenly, we have the opportunity to talk. Things quiet down by Tuesday morning - making the second day of the week perfect to make your announcement or to have a

conversation.

No one is ready for Monday

Office Space clichés aside, we have to do a mental shift after two days off. Even if, like me, you work over the weekend, there's a difference between quietly getting things done and manning the workday phone, email and social media. Respect that you, and most every one else, are still in second gear. Treat Monday as you would Friday: Laying the groundwork for the upcoming days, but leaving the serious thought and actions to later.

No one is listening on Monday

When it comes to connecting with others, Monday is a pretty rough day. Monday is considered one of the weakest days to post on social media (Wednesday, arguably, is the best) as well as one of the worst days to cold call (Friday takes the award here). Save your heavy discussions and your "asks" for another day. Tuesday is an excellent candidate.

No one is satisfied with his or her progress on Monday

As a 5-day culture, we create this immense pressure to be as productive as possible every week. It may motivate you sometimes, but any less than stellar work or unfinished business comes back to bite us in the behind on Monday. It's like the Ghost of Friday's Past begins haunting on Sunday night - and by Monday morning, you are feeling the weight to make up even more for last week's lackluster productivity (even if it isn't actually lackluster). The expectation of bigger, better results can be an internal struggle or, worse, projected onto other people, including employees and colleagues, which means that even if you don't feel that way on Monday, there are others that are struggling. Why not sidestep the melodrama? Make a simple, limited list of what must get done on Monday, create a dialog with others enforcing the focused approach and save the heavy lifting for a less psychologically day: Tuesday.

13

TOO BUSY

Being too busy shows poor business vision

Based on our most common conversations, busyness today is an epidemic--even more so than it was for previous generations with less technology available. In fact, it can be a point of pride.

The truth is that we are not too busy; we just have too many choices to make clear priorities. One of the worst things you can say to someone in business is that you "are too busy."

Unfortunately, other people may be smart enough to understand your real message, even if you don't realize it yourself.

You don't care.
It's OK, as you can't care about everything--the very nature of something being a priority is that other things are less cared about. The first step, though, is to know yourself well enough to understand that you don't really care. The next step is to find a gentle way to say no. Start here.

You are inefficient.
Perhaps the most damning view is that you simply can't handle your business time efficiently. This

perception goes double for fellow entrepreneurs: Many of us launched successful startups while juggling other personal and professional commitments. We're the last people you want to tell "I'm too busy." Instead, explain that you're working hard to give excellent attention to your current projects and, if possible, you will make room for other projects in the future.

You aren't serious about your business.
How many times do successful businesspeople turn down work? Quite often, actually, but it is because of their clarity of focus, not their busy schedule. It is a novice move to burn bridges or close doors prematurely, as your busy season today may turn into a slow churn tomorrow.

14

A Gentle "No"

Saying "no" is more important than saying "yes"

Rejection is a part of business, particularly entrepreneurship, but the biggest, most important rejections have to come from you. You can't accept every offer. You can't pursue every idea. You can't please every customer.

Unfortunately, between our "winner takes all" mentality and our fear of turning away work, we rarely develop the skills necessary to say No. In fact, saying No is easy. Stopping an action without destroying a potential future relationship is hard.

Here are three strong, kind and honest ways to say no--and actually learn about potential collaborators in the process:

"When we work together, I want to make sure you have my full attention."
One of my biggest pet peeves is when a business partner commits to working together, but obviously has too much on his plate. The problem is that I do my best to make sure that I'm not overextended so he gets the attention and details deserved - and I assume others do the same.

"I need to respect those to whom I've already committed."

It reminds me of the adage "If someone gossips to you about other people, you can bet they are gossiping about you to other people." The same could be said for other business dealings: People who are unwilling to say No to you, even though they know they can't give you quality time, are the same people who will willingly sacrifice their commitment to you to work with someone else to whom they can't say No.

A potential collaborator may not like that you are prioritizing others' previous needs over their current needs, but they should respect it. If they don't respect your commitment to others, then that often reflects their own principles - and it may be a warning sign to keep in the back of your mind.

"We should make sure the timing is good."

Your business should naturally evolve, whether it means changing your product scope or identifying a new customer base. It means yesterday's great projects are today's misfires and last year's potential partnerships are now pretty lukewarm. There are amazing collaborators, clients and mentors I would love to work with right now, but as I focus in on my core business, I've had to gently let them know that our time to work together isn't here... yet. It leaves the door open for later opportunities and also confirms that you respect other people's time and are keen not to waste it.

"There's no problem with being where you are right now. We can be where we are and at the same time leave wide open the possibility of being able to expand far beyond where we are now in the course of our lifetime."

-Pema Chodron, Comfortable With Uncertainty

15
EMBRACE LIMITATION
Limited resources foster creativity and genius

I wrote about a dozen books over seven years, so it isn't unusual for others to talk to me about their ambitions to write. Overall I found that the biggest reason people haven't written a book yet is not a lack of literacy, nor the inability to understand publishing (indeed, you can Google self-publishing resources and have a book out by next week). The excuse was always something intangible, that things just hadn't come together yet.

"I haven't found the time.", "I need money to do it right.", "I am not living in the right place to really promote it."

Often, these are lies we tell ourselves. As we discussed in LIES WE TELL, "You will always need more resources than you have, more time than you got and more energy than you can muster. If Jobs, Musk and other visionaries waited until everything was perfect, then we wouldn't be talking about Jobs, Musk and their contemporaries right now."

Those books as well as major consulting gigs and even my last acquired startup were all done under some kind of resource poverty: Time, money or location. Call me crazy, but those actually made the opportunities not only better, but increased the chances of those opportunities actually showing up.

Personal scarcity
Isn't it amazing how we manage to get our projects done just in the nick of time, no matter how long the deadline? We always pace ourselves, expanding and contracting our productivity, based on the time available. Our biggest constraints are often personal: Relationship needs like our families, physical needs like our rest, or emotional needs like our hobbies. After having my first kid, my workweek was slashed from 60 hours to about 15 hours - and I launched two startups, did two TED talks and blossomed my career while being his primary caretaker. It's not about time, but efficiency.

Financial scarcity
We may dream about being billionaires, but complete financial freedom can actually be a detriment to productivity. Artists and entrepreneurs often thrive when they have fewer resources simply because they must be more creative and innovative. Waiting until your money is better is often a mistake.

Location scarcity
It's not about Silicon Valley. I have meet fascinating entrepreneurs in nontraditional areas like

Cincinnati, Detroit, and Miami aiming to put their city on the map or bring it back to past glory. I also know entrepreneurs who are sitting on their laurels until they can move to a major city, which is akin to an author waiting until they meet an agent to type any words. The question is, where can you make the most impact?

16

MARTYRDOM

Sacrificing your well being won't help your business

Passion usually gets us into our entrepreneurial profession, as there would be little other reason for us to take such giant risks. It's a double-edged sword, though, as passion can make us push ourselves too hard. It also can have us make short-term decisions that don't make any sense for our well-being or, ironically, for our actual long-term business.

We should expect to make adjustments within specific periods - people call it "crunch time". For instance, I spent more than a year getting up in the wee hours of the night to launch my startups and my speaking career, but I put a set time limit on that insane schedule, which helped me stay balanced throughout.

Unfortunately, it is way too easy to begin sacrificing important things and making crisis mode your default. Here are the big three parts of your life that are not worth putting at the sacrificial altar.

Sleep

I'm guilty as charged on this one, which is why I can speak from experience. Media mogul Arianna

Huffington has written a best-selling book on the importance of sleep. Jeff Bezos, who is easily controlling half of your online commerce, gets eight hours a night. Science has proven that it is more productive to get more sleep and work less than it is to do the opposite (and why a nap should be on your daily agenda).

Food
A "nutritious" shake may save 15 minutes time, but it doesn't give your mind and body the break it needs to process problems nor to rest between intense work blocks. Not eating at all is truly a recipe for disaster, and the older we get, the less our bodies will tolerate the stress.

Relationships
What's funny is that we never really sacrifice our relationships, but just burn out our social currency. You become the friend that only calls when she needs something (and, as an entrepreneur, you will definitely eventually need something). Not cultivating and managing your relationships ends up hurting your business growth - doing the opposite of what you may claim you're not cultivating and managing your relationships for.

17

SCARY VACATIONS

Never stopping isn't a sign of strength, but of fear

Legendary entrepreneur Elon Musk recently shared a private issue with the press: He is afraid of taking a break. He was quoted as saying:

The first time I took a week off, the Orbital Sciences rocket exploded and Richard Branson's rocket exploded. In that same week, the second time I took a week off, my rocket exploded. The lesson here is don't take a week off.

It may be a brilliantly logical man showing his superstitious side, but his phobia of vacation echoes what many of us believe: You can't afford to stop. Evidence now shows that you can't afford not to stop, but there are many reasons why you believe you can't have or don't deserve a break.

You don't have the structure in place

Have you enabled your business enough so you can actually be unavailable for a few days? Very few of us have. It goes beyond vacation, though: Personally, unexpected health issues and family emergencies have put my own work at a standstill. Enabling co-workers, subordinates, or even our brain trusts is key to feeling better about taking a break. It also requires putting your ego aside and realizing that denying yourself time to recharge doesn't equate "crushing it" as an entrepreneur.

You fear competitors will quickly leave you in the dust

Often in our minds, competitors are No-Doz snorting freaks of nature that never rest. They are just waiting for us to pause so they can take the lead. Even the noblest professions have a ruthless edge, but stopping actually can give our minds the chance to create the strategy we need to win.

The greatest entrepreneur of our generation, Steve Jobs, took infamously long walk breaks. Stopping also prevents us from tinkering too much on our products. Finally, we are less likely to go to extreme thinking and ruin what we've spent so much time building.

You are afraid of facing what you've left behind

Startups can easily demand all of our time, to the point that many of us have given up on having any type of healthy social or family life. But what happens when your business closes or you have a successful exit and you have nothing else to focus on but your life outside of work? It's a scary thought, especially if there is a trail of broken promises and strained relationships laying in your ambitious wake. Unfortunately, avoiding personal conflict just prolongs, if not exacerbates the issues that aren't being addressed. Facing those demons is akin to the popular proverb about planting trees: "The best time to do it would be 20 years ago. The second best time to do it would be today."

When is the last time you actually stopped?

18

THE SMARTEST PERSON
Your network really is your net worth

We create startups with the idealistic intention of building a community around it, yet often don't take the time to create a community within our own personal entrepreneurship. This dawned on me when I was in Silicon Valley and, organically, my friends and I had created our own brain trust.

A hodge podge of techies, entrepreneurs and artists, we'd gather together every week to drink, connect, and recap. It became a magnet, as regulars would inevitably have a friend in town or another colleague interested in coming through and they, too, would stop by whenever possible. The diversity in people pushed our conversations beyond any discussions we could have had in a less public forum.

I left the Bay Area a while ago, but I'm still connected to the valuable people I met. Now we've spun off into interesting ventures, like tackling Silicon Valley diversity and leading the discussion on tech's human impact. More than that, they became the trusted colleagues and mentors for my startup adventures.

In short, they are my brain trust: A diverse, collective sounding board for my next entrepreneurial moves. And every entrepreneur should have one.

Do you have people to listen to your ideas and help you take things to the next level? Here's how you can cultivate them.

Rise to the occasion

As the saying goes, if you're the smartest person in the room, then you need to go find a better room. Your collective should push you to be more strategic, more ambitious and more successful, rather than stroke your ego based on past actions.

Being around smart, accomplished people will push you to higher heights. Attending my first TED Conference was both thrilling and intimidating, but the experience turned me into a regular attendee and, a few years later, a TED speaker myself. Connecting with the American Society of Journalists and Authors made me realize how much further I could go with my writing, inspiring me to become an active member and eventually join its Board of Directors. You should connect with people who help you recognize and encourage you to be your highest self.

Make the time

Our lives can be a blur of late nights/early mornings, airport hopping and crunch times. Cultivating a reliable set of colleagues and mentors should be built into your schedule, just as you would make time for strategic planning or for budget allocation.

Consider the return on investment. I recently offered to take a wise colleague out for an expensive meal. What I got was advice that helped me wrap up my startup gracefully. The priceless insight not only required me setting aside time for the dinner, but also energy building and cultivating the relationship to the point where I could have a long dinner with them. Relationships take time.

Talk to folks in other disciplines

Artists can often be bad businesspeople not because they are awful at math, but because they don't mingle with MBAs and accountants who could give them advice. It is easy to stay in the comfort zone and, as we get older, it gets harder to leave it.

Connecting with different professionals becomes even more important after we get established. Early in our career, we are eager for leads, feedback and direction. As our work stabilizes, though, we think we already have the contacts we need and assume the work will continue to flow. It's not until we need the insight of an advertising specialist, or a media journalist, or another highly-focused professional outside of our field that we realize how narrow our circle has become. You don't want to be facing a difficult business decision and have no one to give you an informed opinion on it.

How are you building a reliable entrepreneurial community for yourself?

19

BE BORED
Not doing encourages daring ideas

We talk today about powering through pain, fatigue, and exhaustion to reach our entrepreneurial goals, but sometimes stopping is exactly what we need to do to understand what we should be doing next. And stopping, sometimes, requires being bored.

Best-selling The Personal MBA author Josh Kaufman explained it well on entrepreneur Tara Gentile's *Profit Power Pursuit* podcast:

I'm actually thinking about taking the Internet out of my office entirely. The more you can make it harder for yourself to focus on anything else, that's valuable. I think there's a lot to be said for "strategic boredom". Just removing all the other things that could be potential distractions... just get rid of them temporarily. And if you can make what you want to do the most interesting thing that you have in your environment, then a lot more gets done that way.

Kaufman calls it "strategic boredom". Whatever you are doing, whether it is a strategy session, a pitch deck or a new manuscript, has to be the most interesting thing happening in your world at that moment. Your social media timeline, mindless busy work and other potential distractions have no place here. Personally, I've found my own work elevated when I minimize the amount of focal points I have - which sometimes means physically unplugging the Internet.

When is the last time you allowed yourself to be bored? If you can't imagine it, then you likely fear it. Here are three reasons why it scares us.

We waste time being afraid of wasting time

Boredom is considered a bad thing today, as we associate it with unproductivity. We always want to feel like we are busy by being on social media, going on business trips, or doing all-nighters for the business. However, our most insightful strategies and ideas happen when we are walking somewhere, taking a moment to think or actually resting for a moment.

In fact, a recent study cited by the Harvard Business Review found that we are more productive when we take time to look at nature. Having been raised in the city, I associated nature with boredom well into adulthood, as perhaps you did, too. As the study shows, though, nature is really a catalyst for us to pause and access the moment. It gives our brains a chance to process and strategize--and avoid potentially time-wasting moves in the future.

We worry that inaction will make things fall apart
The entrepreneurial world seems to operate on two
gears: Stop or Run. You are either running towards
profitability or paddling to stay afloat. It is extreme
thinking, and it is what keeps us willingly
sacrificing our health and our relationships to reach
another business milestone.

Crunch time is real, but insane hours, emotional
stress, and ridiculous malnutrition are meant for
significant stretches, not as the default. Is every
moment crucial? Probably not, or your definition of
crucial isn't really valid. The truth is that our ego
wants to believe that we are sacrificing everything
at this moment because it is what is required of us
to succeed. Working without pause also helps us
avoid boredom, and that very silence that would
make us face the truth about the decisions we've
made and the ones we keep on making.

**We fear we aren't good enough, so we tinker
when we shouldn't**
The fear of boredom also means that we will mess
with things when we really should let them flow
naturally. Picture the nervous artist fussing over a
painting that is already done or a businessperson
aggressively addressing a harmless contractual
point at the last minute. We have the ability to
destroy all our hard work simply because we can't
just sit still and shut up.

Mounting scientific evidence says that creatives--the risk takers and the entrepreneurs--are more likely to overthink their ideas and strategies to the point of neurosis. The deck is already stacked against us. Don't be your own worst enemy.

20

AFTER THE WIN
We are most vulnerable after a success

If we love anything, then it is talking about the struggle to succeed. It is about being focused, about showing up every day and about potentially betting the farm to win.

But what happens after we win? Well, a lot happens.

Entrepreneur Toni Ko felt lost after she sold her cosmetics company to L'oreal for a reported $500 million. Co-founder Marc Lore felt disappointment when his company was acquired by Amazon for $550 million. I went through my own challenges after my popular app, Cuddlr, was acquired.

The toughest part, though, is allowing ourselves to struggle again in our next pursuit. That's why we are more likely to fail after we win big. And it often isn't the positive, swing for the fences failure, but the soul crushing kind. *The Ego is the Enemy* author Ryan Holiday shared exactly why with entrepreneur Tim Ferriss:

Ego is dangerous when you're aspiring to something, no question, but when you are successful and you've built this thing and then you're trying to do your next thing, when you're convinced that everything you touch turns to gold, that's where ego is the most destructive.

It breaks down into a couple reasons. First, your ego, like all of our egos, is insatiable and is hungry for more praise. It is the equivalent of the lab rat being given a sugar cube: It is fine beforehand but, once the sweet treat is introduced, it will get agitated and angry if it doesn't get it again.

We have to train ourselves not to take our success as the default. Instead, the practice of our work should be the default.

Second, you have taken your mastery for granted. Do you remember the first time you started your profession? I started crafting stories when I was a toddler, so I seriously cannot remember when I began narrating to an audience. The longer you've been doing something, the less you remember the pain, struggle and hard work it initially required. It is why you should diversify your social circles and create side hustles to make sure you are not mentally complacent.

The best cure? Always be a beginner at something.

21
WE NEED YOU
No one can duplicate your unique genius

I spent a remarkable amount of time studying astrology, and I blame Kelby, my first "girlfriend". Cresting and ending as a high school summer over-the-phone-only romance, our relationship was mostly talking about how different we were and how, astrologically, we weren't supposed to work. Around that time, I saw Linda Goodman's *Star Signs* on my grandmother's shelf. I read it several times that summer, from top to bottom, and began reading other books about astrology, which led me to Carl Jung, the Myers-Briggs Test, and more sociology.

Many years later, I'm a broke post-grad student living as a freelance writer in Chicago. I get some stuff published, but I can barely make my apartment rent which was decided based on a job opportunity that vanished. As I reached my wits' end, a friend of a friend connected me with a major online portal. It was looking for editorial content and wondered what I could write about. I highlighted technology, video games, sexuality and – screw it – astrology. It immediately hired me as an astrologist, pulling in a salary that I would even consider decent today. And I had some of the most fun ever as a freelancer. I had no idea.

Stuart Butterfield and his partners just made a mint selling the photo website they founded, Flickr, and decided to reinvest some of it into creating a video game company. They wanted to specifically focus on the online experience. Unfortunately, they invested millions into the PC realm right when mobile was rising. Realizing their folly, the founders had a hard conversation with investors and decided to shut down the company. The investors were in deep, too, at least $17 million. The founders had a meeting laying off virtually the entire team, during which Butterfield burst into tears. The founders went back to the drawing board.

While they were working on the game, though, they created an elaborate internal chat system that allowed them to quickly communicate and share files with each other. With nothing to lose, they began sharing the chat system with friends at Microsoft and other companies. The team was surprised at the response and realized that their little side project, not their robust video game, was the real hit. They named it Slack. By Summer 2016, Slack was the defacto corporate chat choice and was worth $4 billion. It was only four years old. Butterfield had no idea.

Let's talk about you. The crazy idea in your head may be the very next thing the world needs. There is no use in waiting for a sign (unless you absolutely need to, which, in that case, consider this your sign.) You can't rely on timing, as it may take you weeks, months, or even years to do your thing, and you have no idea what the world will look like at that moment. You can't rely on others, as no one else shares the exact vision you have, so no one else can tell you whether to go forward or not. And you can't rely on the past, as doing more of what was done yesterday is a waste of all of our time, particularly yours.

What you can do is listen to that nagging voice that is telling you that you have a higher purpose. What you can do is begin moving towards that higher purpose. What you can do is start walking. Today.

Steven Presssfield sums it up well in his classic book *The War of Art*:

"Creative work is not a selfish act or a bit for attention on the part of the actor. It's a gift to the world and every being in it. Don't cheat us of your contribution."

What are you being called to contribute right now?

ON PRODUCTIVITY
(THE PRODUCTIVE BITE-SIZED ENTREPRENEUR)

To Abhi,
whose smile reminds me of the beauty of life itself.
Thank you.

"In fact, there is no inherent problem in our desire to escalate our goals, as long as we enjoy the struggle along the way."

- *Mihaly Csikszentmihalyi, Flow*

HOW NOT TO BE PRODUCTIVE

When I wrote the first THE BITE-SIZED ENTREPRENEUR, my intention was to arm you with everything you needed to find and trust your passion, and use that direction to create your ultimate side hustle.

You and other wonderful readers sent me great feedback about your own personal journeys in entrepreneurship, along with your questions. Lots of questions. I quickly realized that you were hungry for more.

I liken it to going to one of those upscale, gourmet Vegas buffets: You can sample just about anything and everything that a restaurant has to offer, but once you've tried it all, you know what food you really love. Once you know what you prefer, your next move should be going straight to a restaurant that specializes in that dish.

THE PRODUCTIVE BITE-SIZED ENTREPRENEUR is specialty served on a platter. If the first book laid the foundation to ignite your passion, this follow-up is here to help you sustain it. After all, once you make room in your life and grow into your successful side hustle, then your main focus has to be on maintaining and strengthening your business. Your business is always a reflection of yourself. This book will make you a more productive version of yourself.

If you are looking for productivity hacks, then this is probably the wrong book for you. It's actually my fault, not just because I wrote this book you have in your hands, but because I have an aversion to the popular word "hack". Part of it is my background, as, in journalism, a hack is someone who is a lazy writer. Part of it is the second life of my career, as a tech entrepreneur, where a hack is a quick, smart shortcut to a problem.

Here's the issue: There is no shortcut to productivity. There is no hack.

In being around extremely productive people and observing my own most productive periods, I've found that strong productivity is less about banal, universal shortcuts and more about preparing your mindset. In culinary culture, preparers do a mis en place, an organization of their tools, raw foods, and other items, just in the right place so that, when order after order comes in at the heat of the night, they don't need to think about what's next. Smart productivity is the same way. It is instinctive from preparation and habit.

I learned this first hand, as my most productive time wasn't 15 years of working 60 hours a week as a freelance journalist and author, but the three years of working 15 hours a week as a journalist, author, entrepreneur, and speaker after my two sons were born. As I said in THE BITE-SIZED ENTREPRENEUR, "I found myself learning Apple's iPhone programming language with one hand while rocking my newborn in my other, spare arm." The very limitation of time accelerated my productivity, but I also had to be mentally ready to step up my game.

To be the most productive, you have to make room for inspiration, set the plate for action, and give patience for recovery. Keep in mind that inspiration doesn't mean waiting until you feel like doing something, but putting in the proper R & D (research and development) so you are likely to find the creative spark and the strategic genius. Setting the plate is keeping obstacles clear of your momentum. Recovery is respecting your own balance, celebrating your progress, and assessing your next move.

Being productive every single day is a fruitless goal. To maximize productivity, you have to accept that you will not be able to give 100% every single moment of your life. Constantly working means you aren't taking time to integrate lessons learned during action, just as much as staying idle means you aren't testing theories in your head.

Productivity is a cycle, not a sprint.

I call the productivity process "pursuing, doing, and renewing". It is an infinite iterative flow where we research our interests, implement our theories, and assess our growth. It is not unlike Eric Ries' landmark Lean Startup method, in which you ship the "minimal viable product", or MVP, to get feedback from others as much as possible. In the case of productivity, we're getting feedback from ourselves.

THE PRODUCTIVE ENTREPRENEUR is broken down into three sections loosely based on the process: Pursuing, Doing, and Renewing. Like other THE BITE-SIZED ENTREPRENEUR books, you can read the strategies in any order, but your productivity will be much stronger if you go through it from top to bottom. If you are new to entrepreneurial pursuits, it also may be worthwhile reading the original THE BITE-SIZED ENTREPRENEUR to get a solid foundation for the basics.

It would be indulgent to spend more time laying the groundwork for a book on productivity, so let's get started. Enjoy!

-Damon Brown, September 2016

I: Pursuing

"At the beginning of any new idea, the possibilities can seem infinite, and that wide-open landscape of opportunity can become a prison of anxiety and self-doubt."

-Peter Sims, Little Bets

1

CREATE LIMITATIONS
You automatically take as much time as you are given

It began with getting up at 5 a.m. That was the plan. Our baby would wake up at 6, and, since I was the primary caretaker at home, I'd be able to get a sufficient amount of business done before then. I quickly learned that meant I didn't shower unless he took a nap, so I started getting up at 4:30 a.m. Then I realized I couldn't make morning tea or coffee unless I got up at 4:15 a.m., and that I had to refuse my steadily increasing workload unless I woke up at 4:00 a.m.

The scales kept adjusting until I found a new wakeup time: 3:15 a.m. It was an hour after the bar's last call, making it officially morning. Three o' clock still carries the smell and the silence of the night, though, and it gave me the isolation and darkness that fueled my creativity. I traded my extreme late nights of younger years for very productive mornings. I had space.

My son became my end-of-day clock, and when he rang around 6 a.m., I had usually already talked to my New York contacts, written an article, and tackled a new business strategy for my first app, So Quotable. The time shift became invaluable when I launched my app Cuddlr, not only because my main co-founder was in the U.K., but later when I needed significant time to steer its significant userbase and eventual acquisition.

Around the time of my change, I caught a popular article that said we used to sleep in two shifts as recently as a couple centuries ago.

[Virginia Tech History professor Roger Ekirch] found that we didn't always sleep in one eight hour chunk. We used to sleep in two shorter periods, over a longer range of night. This range was about 12 hours long, and began with a sleep of three to four hours, wakefulness of two to three hours, then sleep again until morning.

That was all I needed to hear. "Maybe this temporary thing will work...forever!" I told myself one morning before sunrise.

After several months, however, I realized that this should not – or rather, could not – be my default. My moods began swinging. My body began to ache.

I told myself to hang in there, that I'd keep at it for a year. As the 12th month arrived on the horizon, I hit the equivalent of a runner's wall, and I limped to the finish line.

Clearly, it was time for a change. I decided to look

at my priorities. I started saying no to gigs, accepted that parts of my to-do list wouldn't get done, and gave myself at least one alarm-free morning every week. The aches went away, my mind cleared up, and everything became more focused. The year following this experiment was even more productive, as I zeroed in on only the projects about which I was most passionate – simply because I didn't have the time to do anything else.

My years of working at odd hours and [insert chuckle here] "waiting to be inspired" to create were replaced by a stable, disciplined regiment. In an instant, my 60-hour-work week was sliced down to 15 hours a week. I viewed myself as a marathon runner doing a daily, three-hour leg.

My first year as a parent became one of the most productive years of my life.

Have you ever found yourself more productive when you have less time? It reminds me of an old programming adage: Programmers always manage to get things done with just the amount of computer memory they are given. It's the same reason why we always seem to spend through the money we have, or feel like we complete things just before the deadline is about to strike. We automatically take as much space as we are given.

When we are aware of how much little time we

have, though, we begin compressing. As Brain Pickings' Maria Popova shared in a recent article, our relative view of time slows down when we feel threatened. In this case, the threat could be not getting the last sentence down in an idea or not sending out that client email before you run out of time. You realize how many minutes you spend checking social media, fixing a snack, or gazing out of the window. Those moments of disengagement can become the quiet time killers that keep you from being more efficient.

I learned this rather recently. In my compressed work year, I did my first TED talk, gave a keynote speech at American University, programmed and designed my first app, made TV appearances on Al Jazeera America and other outlets, and joined multiple startup advisory boards – all while being my first son's primary caretaker while still maintaining an active writing career. Not only was I driven by passion for both my family and my work, but also by my acute awareness that time was limited. My proverbial alarm clock was going to wake up around 6 a. m., which, from 3 a. m., gave me about 180 minutes each day to get my passion projects accomplished.

Here are some thoughts on how to maximize your time:

Monotasking

As I discuss in my book *Our Virtual Shadow: Why We Are Obsessed with Documenting Our Lives Online*, scientific studies now prove multitasking doesn't really exist. What we view as multitasking is just picking up one task, dropping it quickly for another task, and then repeating the same process over and over again until they are both done. Instead, concentrate on getting one thing done well. The completion will boost your energy-and focus-for the next item on your list.

Return on investment

Forget the money ROI – what is your time ROI? We lose the most time by wasting it on items that shouldn't be high on our priority list. For all the great opportunities I fulfilled during my compressed year, I said "No" to even more opportunities than I accepted. I still do.

Slice and dice

In her book *Six-Figure Freelancing*, Kelly K. James talks about breaking the day up into 15-minute segments. This former lawyer gets things done by essentially giving herself a time limit for her work.

Time, not money, is an entrepreneur's most precious resource. A life change taught me this lesson, but you shouldn't wait for that to happen.

2

DEVELOP YOUR CORE
Do many things with one purpose

Have you noticed that the most productive people usually aren't exhausted? I mean, they get tired, but you rarely see them ready to pass out in a random corner or forced to take a mandatory vacation based on doctors' orders. On the other hand, those who seem the most stressed and burnt out seem to get things done within a hair of failure. If the wind blew the wrong way, you'd expect them just to topple over right where they once stood.

You can point to personality, disposition, or stamina, but I believe it comes down to one special difference: Focus. The most productive people are focused, usually on one priority. The least productive people are focused on many things, usually on many priorities, which, of course, means that nothing really is a priority. It is multitasking versus monotasking and diffused energy versus concentrated energy. Have you ever taken a magnifying glass and made a pinpoint with the rays of the sun until smoke started to rise? Productive people bring that level of concentration to their goals.

It gets confusing, though, when the most popular productive people seem to be spread so damn thin. For every creative like Jiro Ono, the singular-focused master chef featured in the film *Jiro Dreams of Sushi*, there are lots more like Richard Branson, the multimedia mogul who has built music, movies, airlines, and even spaceships under his Virgin brand. Oprah Winfrey, Jeff Bezos, and others always seem to have a new venture, yet never seem to be as stretched as much as the average Joe multitasking through his relatively simple life.

The truth is that Jiro and Richard and Oprah and Jeff are the same. Their expressions are obviously different, but they all have one simple, clear intention to their career. That's why it is absolutely crucial that you say "No" as often as possible. Can you imagine how many times Jiro said "No" to expanding beyond his small, exclusive restaurant (watch the movie to get a better idea), or the few number of times Oprah actually says "Yes" to a new project idea?

The beautiful part is that each of these successful individuals instinctually knows what next step for their business should likely be and what would be a misfire – simply because they have taken the time to know themselves and, therefore, found their purpose. Why do you do want to do what you do? If you want to be the most productive, then you have to know your end game.

And, in a Zen-like paradox, the better you know yourself, the less options you have to grow, as everything won't be for you, but the more narrow that focus, the more productive you will be in the areas that you *do* care about.

One of my favorite analogies is from Martha Stewart's *The Martha Rules*. My mentor Andrea King Collier told me about the following excerpt years ago. It ended up changing the course of my career:

We once [listed] all of our media platforms and traced how the little pansy flower had been covered in each one: Our magazine featured cupcakes decorated with sugared pansies; on television, I demonstrated how to apply pressed pansies onto paper, creating lovely stationary; on my daily radio show, I explained to listeners that the word pansy *stands for thought and remembrance; the syndicated newspaper column described how to press and dry pansies...*

And she keeps going! For the media mogul, productivity didn't mean reinventing the wheel to feed her many, many platforms, but taking one core idea and adapting it to each audience. My "pansy" is intimacy and technology, which turned me into a tech culture journalist, a speaker on human connection, and, most recently, the founder of a tech app that facilitated person-to-person intimacy. I'm happy with how my career has gone so far, but it also meant saying "No" to opportunities that would have derailed my journey or diluted my focus.

At the beginning of any new opportunity, the possibilities can seem infinite, and that seemingly exciting wide-open landscape of opportunity can turn into a prison of anxiety and self-doubt. Forget losing productivity; If you get too overwhelmed, you might end up losing yourself.

Learning, developing, and protecting your core is key to being the most productive entrepreneur possible. You should be able to say it in one short sentence, like an elevator pitch cut in half.

Do you know your core?

3

DEATH BY NETWORKING
You can only talk about an idea so much

I just did something I hadn't done in a while: I went to a networking event. The more time passes, the more I get out of connecting within organic environments and, occasionally, bonding at a small conference. Besides, with now two young kids and a busy business, I don't have much time.

During the cocktail hour, I chatted with an older gentleman, a serial entrepreneur. He asked me if I knew the scene, as he didn't know anyone. I was puzzled, then relieved as I admitted that I hadn't been to a networking event in a while.

We then both realized that we had been too busy *doing* rather than *talking*.

Networking is absolutely important: It grows your brain trust, exposes you to new ideas and gives you a break from the day-to-day grind. But going regularly specifically to networking events has an effect of diminished returns, especially if you are going to them within the same circles. Are you starting to recognize the same people at networking events? Then it's probably time to stop.

One of the great things about parenthood and other

external responsibilities is that it forces you not to waste time. Back in Silicon Valley, I would spend hours every week at networking events - as did most people I knew. Mind you, I didn't do the TED Talks, startups, and bigger books until after I left the Silicon Valley networking scene, started a family, and took my time more seriously. I don't think that's a coincidence.

Before I go to an event, networking or otherwise, I ask myself one question:

Is there something more productive I could be doing with this time?

No wonder I, a travel and connecting fanatic, have only gone to only two conferences this year. With all that "extra" time, I wrote a book. I implore you to ask yourself the same question.

4
WRITE IT DOWN
Ideas go on paper, not on keyboard

Paper is definitely down in popularity, as we are more likely to open up a note application or send a quick email to ourselves than to physically write down something. Even classic journals like Moleskine are going digital.

It's all the more reason to check out NPR's recent interview of two University of California, Los Angeles researchers comparing students' handwritten note taking versus typed out notes. The results were stunning:

"When people type their notes, they have this tendency to try to take verbatim notes and write down as much of the lecture as they can," Mueller tells NPR's Rachel Martin. "The students who were taking longhand notes in our studies were forced to be more selective -- because you can't write as fast as you can type. And that extra processing of the material that they were doing benefited them."

The scientists found that laptop and written note-takers were equal when it came to facts and figures, but laptop note takers did "significantly worse" when it came to internalizing concepts.

The prevailing theory is this: When you write something by hand, your brain actually has to process the information because it is often not possible to write down every thing being said. Typing, on the other hand, lends itself to speed. You are more likely to try to capture every word rather than jot down the intent.

It is not practical, if impossible to write down everything by hand, but there are some key situations where writing would be more effective than typing:

- Capturing a lecture or presentation
- Preparing for your own lecture or presentation
- Documenting an initial business meeting to set expectations
- Creating a framework for your new business idea

I did a TED Talk on the power of writing our big ideas on little pieces of paper. It doesn't have to be on a little piece of paper, though. It can be on whatever you wish. It is the manual act of writing itself that is valuable.

Today we default to texting something into our smartphone or whipping out the laptop, but we often forget the power of handwriting. Here is why you should consider writing your next thoughts down instead of typing them out.

Filter your thoughts

We go through a filtering process when we write things down. If you're like me, you can type much faster than you can write--and the additional time and energy required to move your pen means you are more thoughtful in what you capture on the page. It's not limited to words, either: Doing a quick sketch or diagram can sometimes be the key to focusing your thoughts and expressing hard-to-articulate ideas.

Remember what you were thinking

I write everything down on an index card whenever I have a big idea or need to work something out, as cards are compact, portable and efficient. Some of my index card ideas are rubbish, but the ones that are the most valuable eventually get put in a recipe box. (Thankfully, post-TED Talk, they are no longer all over my office.) Now I can access brainstorms or thoughts I had months, even years ago--and they are often strong ideas I would have long forgotten. It's like having a Google for my brain.

Articulate the abstract

Consider it an elevator pitch to yourself. While ideas are broad and encompassing, words are limiting and linear. Use this to your advantage: Find the right language to express your next product or venture. Writing out your thoughts takes them out of your head and forces you to capture them in a cohesive manner without potential distractions or aids like PowerPoint, spellcheck or the World Wide Web. Your scribbles can be both raw in concept and structured in words--a powerful combination.

When is the last time you tried writing down your thoughts, rather than typing things out, to get through an impasse or to work out a strategy?

5
EMPTY YOUR SCHEDULE
Scheduling a blank day boosts productivity

One of the safest things you can do personally is overcommit yourself. It is also perhaps the worst thing you can do to your business. The security of proving how busy you are and using busyness as a gauge for success will ultimately drop the quality of your interactions, your service and your health. Fighting to be the busiest entrepreneur in the room is an arms race you don't want to win.

My personal cure for overscheduling is to simply schedule a blank day. It doesn't even have to be an entire day. On a regular basis, I will set aside four to 12 hours dedicated to bettering my mind. My phone goes to voicemail, my email is paused, and meetings are pushed to a later date.

These aren't vacation days, but days of self-driven thought, productivity and realignment. Imagine what you could do with a scheduled day of betterment?
- Modify your business plan
- Catch up on must-read materials
- Call previous clients to reconnect

An "unscheduled" day is integral to my business, but it can feel awkward when you first try it. Here's how you can make your own blank day.

Schedule
Yes, you need to schedule your blank day, particularly if you have other people looking at your calendar. Block off the time. Setting it up like a regular meeting trains you to take the blank time seriously. For me, seeing it on my calendar makes me anticipate that day and gives me something to look forward to.

Commit
It is tempting to schedule one or two regular work activities, but even a brief retreat back into your daily grind can take you out of the zone. Instead, commit to the time away just as you would if you were on a Wi-Fi free plane, or sitting in a place with poor cell phone reception, or spending quality time with a loved one. In other words, your office is officially closed for the day.

Maximize
Once you realize your day is open, the possibilities will begin to emerge. Remember, it's not a day of rest, but a day of gathering your mental resources without outside commitments. For me, my blank days are when I finish books, go for thoughtful walks and catch up with dormant clients. They are days to restrategize, retool and recommit. It is me sharpening my axe so I can be a more effective warrior.

6
WHEN TO LET IT GO
Knowing when to stop working is just as important

Except for death and parenting, few things inspire as many quotations and axioms as entrepreneurship. They usually encourage us to keep going: "Fight another day," "It is darkest before the dawn," "Failure just eliminates another bad option," and so on.

Other people need encouragement to keep going. Entrepreneurs, though, need encouragement to *stop*. We're too motivated as it is. Anyone who enters the odds-adverse entrepreneurial world has to be, on some level, an optimist. If anything, we push when we should be still and we goad when we should be receptive. In fact, as discussed in the original THE BITE-SIZED ENTREPRENEUR, our restlessness can destroy something that is already on its way to success.

In my experience, there are three great reasons not to make any more moves on an opportunity:

The launch date/commitment time is already here
Legend has it that Alex Haley's publisher had to send a representative to the author's house to literally pull the *Roots* manuscript out of his hands.

102

As this famed African saga was inspired by Haley's family tree, the author could have kept adding more and more details. But it was too late.

You have a commitment to excellence, but you have a bigger commitment to serve your audience. A great product or service is useless if it never ships.

You did everything you could

Sometimes, there are flaws, challenges, or gaps in what we are presenting, but there is absolutely nothing we can do about it. I experience this regularly in the journalism world, where external factors like page layout, the publication date, and budgetary constraints can severely affect the end result. It is a lesson in doing the best you can... and letting go.

It is in someone else's hands

The roughest part of entrepreneurship, at least for me, isn't the ideation/creation phase, nor the so-called crunch time before launching a product, but the gap where you wait for someone else's response. It could be the audience after a launch, or a partner after you made a big decision, or even a vendor once an important request was submitted. You know the result is important, but there is nothing more for you to do.

Everyone has a method of calming his or her inner

control freak. My regular process is talking out loud through the various scenarios and having a plan A, B, and C in place. For me, having my next chess moves planned calms things down. And, once feedback is given, I'll know exactly what move I should start executing.

7
WALK IT OUT
Get on your feet to recharge your productivity

It has been a turbulent summer of sorts for many of us, with the political unrest, stock market volatility and crazy, dangerous weather. I've been dealing with my own unique stress, reflecting on my anniversary escaping Hurricane Katrina, selling my popular app Cuddlr, and transitioning out of a 3 a.m. daily work routine.

So, one day recently, I just got up from my computer, left the house and started walking. Probably about four miles that day.

I've always loved walking, particularly when I lived in the heart of San Francisco, where it would be a rare day when I didn't walk to tech functions throughout the evening (the city is seven by seven miles, so walking everywhere isn't an unrealistic accomplishment). I then moved to Southern California in which most cities, unlike New York, Chicago and D.C., aren't conducive to walking everywhere. I also started a family, and those hours spent walking-or hours spent doing anything-seemed as impractical as they seemed wasteful. But now I'm taking the time to walk, whether it be in the morning or in the night, as I'm realizing it is how I clear my mind and how I process my day. It has been like a meditation, though many of us who do walk regularly may not even realize the positive impact it has on our mental balance.

Walking for clarity isn't a revolutionary idea. According to *The Last Great Walk* author Wayne Curtis, the health benefits of regular walking came into view about a century ago-particularly when it came to keeping ourselves young.

What is new is that entrepreneurs are actually starting to value it. Consultant Nilofer Merchant has a short, excellent TED talk on why business people should take walking seriously. As we spend more time on tech and less time taking care of ourselves, I tend to agree.

Here's how you can incorporate walking into your daily entrepreneurial life.

Do walking meetings

Walking can be an excellent time to take conference calls, especially those that have you mostly on mute. If you are fortunate enough to work near your colleagues, take them with you on a brief jaunt. It may help you work out knotty ideas or even ease the tension of a particularly sensitive conversation-Steve Jobs famously had his most important discussions on his feet.

Get smart

It is also a great opportunity to listen to business books or, on the free side, to podcasts. I now listen to Startup, Will Lucas' Of10, and other favorite entrepreneurial podcasts almost exclusively during my walks. It not only makes the time more valuable, but it assuages any guilt that I'm out of the office.

Keep it brief

A walk doesn't have to be an extreme, epic journey-it could be walking to a farther coffee shop for your morning drink or spending an extra 10 minutes taking the long way to lunch. You can look at the additional time as a brief reprieve from the constant device buzz.

Track your walks

If you're into measurable results, consider utilizing a wearable, whether it be a FitBit or Apple Watch, or an old-school pedometer. The ability to see how many steps or miles you've walked can help encourage you to keep going and, perhaps, walk even further the next time you go out.

8
STOP MEASURING TIME
Never mistake time for commitment

Time is often how we measure our commitment to an idea. Someone who put in 20 years developing something successful is looked at as persistent, visionary, and patient. On the other hand, calling someone an "overnight success" is usually a backhanded complement, as it shows a person who potentially got lucky or stumbled upon a brilliant idea. The quick ride to success is looked at with both admiration and envy. They didn't earn their stripes.

The one important thing time does not measure is commitment. Side hustlers, folks that take time outside of their main gig to take their passion seriously, can easily be more committed than full-timers. Can you imagine taking time away from your rest, your leisure, and your life outside of your full-time job to make your dream a reality? Perhaps you can. Perhaps you are doing that right now.

Time spent does not indicate passion nor focus, hence it not equating commitment. Social scientists are now poking holes in the 10,000 hours theory made popular in Malcolm Gladwell's influential *Outliers*. Gladwell argued that mastery of a particular skill happens when someone puts in 10,000 hours of study and practice, citing Bill Gates, The Beatles, and other modern icons. The rub, though, is that we don't know how *focused* people were during those 10,000 hours. Picture Salvador Dali spending countless days doing still life and never progressing into the abstract, disturbing art for which he is known. He was fully present during those proverbial 10,000 hours, and that gave him the vision to create beyond the literal bread and baskets that he painted early in his career. Again, time does not equate *quality time*.

Instead, as Dali went abstract, The Beatles went psychedelic, and Gates went visionary, you should measure your productivity by your evolution. Your growth could be a radical, public departure. Your growth could be a subtle shift inside. It doesn't matter.

As spiritual writer Pema Chodron puts it, "In order to go deeper, there has to be a wholehearted commitment. You begin the warrior's journey when you choose one path and stick to it. Then you let it put you through your changes."

Focus on transformation based on what you are doing, not on the time you spend doing it.

II: DOING

"The professional does not wait for inspiration; he acts in anticipation of it."

-Steven Pressfield, Turning Pro

9

DO LESS WITH MORE IMPACT
Being productive every day is a fool's errand

If busyness is our number one obsession today, then constant productivity is a close second. I'm part of the problem: I not only analyze how some of the most interesting leaders stay focused, but I am obsessed with being productive myself. I had my Masters by my very early 20's and wrote 18 books in the past decade. I've got my own issues.

So perhaps you'll listen when I say this: *You are not meant to be productive all the time.* We seem to think that there is some magic formula that turns our mushy, balanced-oriented human brains into tough, binary computers. There is not.

The best way to be productive is to let yourself be less productive.

Take it one goal at a time
It's no coincidence that some of the most recognized entrepreneurs ruthlessly focus on one thing at a time. Focusing on multiple things doesn't make us get more done, but simply makes us less productive in several areas.

Focus in intervals
I call them palate cleansers, after the refresher you

eat or drink between meal courses. The idea is to focus on something for a short, intense period of time, then to give yourself a break.

Break early, break often

Walking, quiet time, blank days, Internet unplugging, and other disconnections do marvelous things to your productivity because your brain will continue to problem solve while you take in the quiet.

If you really want to get amazing things done, then trade in busyness for productivity. And that happens best in intense cycles, not in breathless marathons.

10

THE NECESSARY THING
Sometimes you can only do one thing well

When I was burning the candle in the middle (well beyond burning it at both ends) and considering giving up, one of my mentors, Rosemary Taylor, gave me a simple directive.

"Chop wood, carry water."

In other words, sometimes the best thing you can do is do the routine, the necessary thing, that needs to be done at the moment, and concentrate on absolutely nothing else. Focus on the first thing, the necessary thing, and then go to the next thing on the list.

That's it. And that is enough for today.

11

ALTERNATE TASKS

Palate cleansers can refresh your focus and productivity

As an entrepreneur, I tend to run hot and cold. I'm burning the midnight oil for weeks, then I have several days where my intensity and, seemingly, my passion seems to dissipate. Unfortunately, that means wasting excess energy when all the work is done and potentially not being as thorough as possible when the energy is low. I know the extreme decision-making trap firsthand.

One practice that helps immensely is palate cleansing. You are taking something to wash away the previous experience to make way for the next one. Mint, bread, and even plain old water are popular palate cleansers, but what if you applied it to your daily actions? Here's food for thought.

Focus on something else
In food, a palate cleanser is usually a light drink or snack that makes your senses focus on something else. It serves as a bridge between two courses. The courses themselves are usually strong or intense. The palate cleanser serves as a break between two extreme experiences, helping you digest the former and get prepared for the latter.

The irony is delicious, here: The more focus you want, the more you need to step away.

Make time to rebuild your focus

I love deep diving into work, but intensity, by its very nature, is in limited quantity. In fact, researchers estimate that you can only hold your complete attention onto something for a couple of hours. (It's the reason why public speakers follow the adage, "Say what you're going to tell them, tell them what you're going to tell them, and then tell them what you just told them.")

It is the reason why it doesn't make much sense to do a 20-hour day with little or no breaks: Your productivity will drop, sooner rather than later, and you may actually be wasting time rather than maximizing it. The 25-minute Pomodoro Technique is the epitome of short focus, but even a 15-minute break every hour or two would be much more efficient than creating a marathon day.

Give room for thought

Why do palate cleansers make you more productive? While you may have checked out, your brain is still focused on the previous project and creating smarter strategies for you to use when you start again. As I recently talked about, resting may be our most powerful entrepreneurial tool. People in traditional lines of work usually can't build their own schedule from scratch! It is a perk that may have gotten us into entrepreneurship, but something we tend to forget after we become entrepreneurs.

A short, daily meditation is my palate cleanser, as is going for a walk and, whenever possible, taking a brief nap. Yours may be checking social media, doing a quick exercise or reaching out to a colleague for a quick chat. We all should find ways to take our ostrich-like heads out of the sand.

12

Overextending Yourself
Burning out doesn't have to happen

It is remarkably easy to do too much, particularly when you love what you do. Does work not feel like work? You may be fortunate enough to be in that situation, but that also means you are less likely to know when you are tilting towards burnout, physically in need of rest, or pushing yourself too hard. Entrepreneurs may have more passion around their career than most, so we are more susceptible to losing ourselves in the excitement of work.

Self-care is a part of taking care of our business, because if we break down, then our business will break down, too. Here are some solid ways to help stave off overextension.

Wait to commit
We feel pressure to say "Yes" to opportunities right away because we're afraid of missing the boat or, worse, our measured response will scare away the person who's offering the opportunity itself. I've found that some opportunities are fleeting, but the number is nowhere near the number of opportunities that we think are fleeting. In other words, when it comes to determining the rarity of an opportunity, we tend to sit on the paranoid side.

Unfortunately, that means we are more likely to say "Yes" to things even when we don't have the resources to take them on. And... suddenly we're overextended.

Instead, try taking a moment to consider letting go of the opportunity being offered. It could be five minutes, it could be an entire evening. Give yourself as much space as can be allotted. You may be surprised at the new considerations that suddenly pop up, ideas that would not have otherwise crossed your mind until, perhaps, it was too late.

Check your gut

Some opportunities can feel particularly rare because they are actually a little too ideal. Fortunately, our gut can give us the warning that we should look deeper. For myself, I may get a feeling that someone is holding back information or that the deal may end up in a different place than intended. It is often right, but the most important part to understand is that your gut isn't specific - it just realizes when something feels off with a situation. And it very well may be telling you that a new opportunity will be too much of a strain on your resources.

Ask a colleague

Sometimes the one to help you stay in check is a trusted confidant. If you have your brain trust in order, then you already have people around you who know your goals, your intentions and your weaknesses. An objective party can warn you when you are veering off your path or potentially falling prey to one of your blind spots.

Look back a year from now
One of the best ways to prevent overextending yourself is to envision how you'd like to spend your time, energy, and focus a year from now. What will you be doing? How will you be doing it? What seeds do you need to plant to get there?

There are few reality checks bigger than realizing the work you are doing now won't get you to where you want to be. No one intends to be unproductive towards his or her dreams. It's just that, when we overextend ourselves, we are too overcommitted and scattered to prioritize the things that will move us closer to our goal over the busy work we're already doing. Think about where you want to go and plan on saying "No" to plans that don't move you forward. "No" should be your default, and seemingly nonessential opportunities should have to be important enough to convince you otherwise.

13
MASTERING TIME
How you can maximize your schedule

Time management master Laura Vanderkam has written several books, including the best-seller *168 Hours*, on how even the most in-demand leaders maintain incredible productivity. She and I agree that the most precious resource you have isn't money, but time.

I got a chance to connect with Vanderkam when she spoke at the recent American Society of Journalists and Authors conference. She shared three master tips to strong time management.

Write down how you spend your time
Create a time journal, not unlike people concerned with their eating habits create a food journal. How can you maximize your time if you aren't sure how you're really spending it?

Vanderkam admitted that she thought she worked 60 hours a week but, after keeping a time journal for several months, realized it was closer to 40 hours a week. By keeping a journal, you can squeeze out the inefficiencies and better understand why you may not feel as productive as you think you should be.

Do a (time) portfolio review

Do a portfolio review of how you spend your time, just like you would for stock performance. In this case, however, you are looking at the allocation of your time assets. Are you spending 10 percent of your time sending and tracking invoicing? Then we're talking five to six weeks out of every year.

Vanderkam found that virtual assistants, interns and smart software can help immensely - and the financial outlay pales compared to the time you save. How else could you be growing your business with the proverbial 10 percent of your year you'd get back?

Done is better than perfect

The ultimate time suck is perfection. Spending too much time perfecting a product or service not only can hurt your business, but it can create opportunity cost for the other great, new things you could be working on.

Vanderkam highly recommends this: "Let it go. Done is better than perfect." Think about the last time you spent an inordinate amount of time for an incremental improvement on a completed project. Now imagine all the other things you could have been doing with that time. At a certain point, spending more time on something will provide significantly diminished returns. Being honest about when you reach that point is perhaps the toughest, most important skill in great time management.

14

PUT THE COFFEE DOWN
Drinking coffee at the wrong time will hurt your day

Unlike many entrepreneurs, I didn't drink coffee through school, nor in young adulthood, and it didn't keep me going during business all nighters and crunch times (adrenaline did that). No, I didn't fall in love with coffee until well into my grown-up life when I began appreciating its bitter, robust flavor.

Thankfully, it was just before taking on a 3 a.m. schedule, but the energy boost has always been a perk, not a reason.

Culturally we usually have coffee first thing in the morning, but I realized that it was much more powerful and effective when I had it later in the day--like 11 a.m. The days went smoother and I focused better. Now science is backing it up, though there are many reasons to hold off on that first cup of java.

Your body doesn't need coffee early
Your body begins pumping cortisol when you wake up in the morning, kind of like a smelling salt to help you rise and shine. The boost happens between 8 a.m. – 9 a.m., followed by other boosts

125

midday and in late afternoon. Drinking coffee first thing in the morning is like adding lighter fluid to an already-growing fire: You quickly burn extra bright, and you burn out just as fast.

However, drinking a cup between 9:30 a.m. to 11:30 a.m. provides an energy bridge between your early cortisol rises. Around 11 a.m. is my sweet spot. It is also important to put the science in context: 8 a.m. was once the perfect time for me to have coffee, but that was when I was waking up at 3:15 a.m., so 8 a.m. was my midday cup.

Coffee can mask your true entrepreneurial feelings

For a caffeine-sensitive person like myself, coffee can make one feel like everything is coming together: You're being super productive, ideas are coming easily, and business is going in the right direction! All the above may or may not be true, but I want to feel that way because of the passion for my business or the rewards of a hard-earned strategy, not because a bean is making me feel brilliant.

As a stimulant, coffee can make us excited about awful ideas, abrasive about our opinions and unable to settle down (or perhaps that's just me!). It can bring out the opposite skills we need to be the best entrepreneur we can be. The potential issue is compounded when we drink it when our bodies are already revving up for the day. Overdoing the coffee first thing in the morning can have us starting the day making bad decisions.

It breaks up your day
The 3 p.m. drag is real, particularly after a heavy lunch, but late morning is often when we really begin to slow down from the rush. The average work day starts with a 6 a.m. jolt of the alarm, the body shock of shower water, the dash for the train or car, the social stimulation of people or traffic and the productivity burst with the intent of catching up or getting things done early in the day. In other words, you're running a sprint until lunch is on the horizon. No wonder we slow down at lunch and need a nap around 2ish.

The 11 a.m. coffee creates a natural break in the day--the transition from sunrise to sunset. On more mellow days, I'll replace my late morning coffee with a strong tea or fruit-infused water. When I do coffee, though, I take it a step further and make it a physical transition by making my coffee by hand with a French press. It takes about five minutes, grinding the beans, pouring in the hot water and pushing down the stopper. For me, it is like a meditation on what I already got done today and what I will get done later. It is a thoughtful pause.

15

KNOW YOUR PRIME TIME
Everyone peaks at different moments

When I was young, my golden hours were from 1 o'clock until dawn. It was something about the silence of the night, the gap between bedtime and rise, that turned me alive. I'd have all kinds of ideas. My writing would flow. An optimistic glaze would cover my world. It wasn't until I couldn't stay up all night (hello, family) that I realized how much my creativity was fueled by certain rituals - and, in this case, certain schedules.

I recently heard the term "golden hours" from People Matters founder Jodi Wehling. I take it as more than just your most productive time of the day. No, it's when you are at your peak in creativity, vision and inspiration - even without a cup of coffee. Here Wehling describes them:

Pay attention over the next week and identify when your best work hours are.

Then guard them with your life. Block the time and mark it as "busy". Resist the temptation to book this time for a meeting.

This is your time. It is worth twice as much as other times in terms of what you can get accomplished.

As a leader, it is terribly easy to let outside forces dictate your schedule. If you get more successful, then defending your own needs becomes harder, not easier.

There are two great, actionable ways to make your golden hours work:

Say no

Nope. Uhn-uh. Can't right now. I recently talked about three smart, strategic ways to say no and save your relationships. Denying people access to you 24/7 is the only way you can preserve your productivity.

Create a blank day

Block off an entire day and make no meetings, phone calls or messaging available. Not only will it give you the space to think, which we rarely create, but it also will give a glimpse into when your golden hours actually are. Undisturbed, I'm productive mid morning, mid afternoon and late evenings, which is much different than when I started my career or even during my early morning rituals a couple years ago. Having a blank day will show you your natural productivity patterns *at this moment.*

Save your energy

Bracket your golden hours with less intensive activities. For instance, if I have meetings or interviews, I place them before or after my most productive moments. It is a great way to preserve your outside work needs and protect your golden hours.

When are your golden hours?

16

THE HARDEST 1%
The last step is by far the most dangerous

I launched my first app, So Quotable, after many years of development, with the app's programmer abandoning the project at the last minute, and four months of learning Apple programming language in the wee hours while taking care of my first son. It was brutal. It launched as a workable, functional product just in time for my first TED talk. I showed it with a mixture of pride and shame, as I could quite see the bubble gum and duct tape that kept it together. I knew it inside and out, so I knew all of its flaws.

Shortly after launch, I showed it with trepidation to a professional, successful programmer who knew my journey. He paused wordlessly for a moment, then gave this big smile.

"I'm impressed!"

"Ha! It's pretty damn rough. What are you impressed by?"

"You shipped."

He knew, I knew, and now you know a secret: You will never want to ship. What you create will never be good enough for the public. If you are doing your job right, then you can name at least five things you would change about the thing you are about to give the world. If you aren't insecure about your next big reveal, then you are either lazy or lying.

Artists don't create. Artists ship. Wrote something that you never show to another soul? You just made a diary entry, not a novel. Make a brilliant product that is stuck in almost done? You just created an amazing demo, not something people can actually use. At this point, your influence will be nil. To paraphrase motivational speaker Steve Harvey, you'll be safe, but you'll never soar.

Off the top of my head, I know several talented people who thrive in the 99% zone: brilliant artists, founders, and creatives – nay, *aspiring* artists, founders, and creatives – who charge like a wrecking ball towards their goals. And then, just as the final piece comes into place, they stop. I bring this up not from a place of judgment, but just to show you how deadly that final 1% can be for anyone creative. The dream of what could be is a strong, seductive opiate compared to the cold reality of your realized idea, filled with bumps and bruises and compromises and constraints, exposed to the elements of criticism and judgment.

It's never starting an idea that shows you are

132

serious about your commitment. It is finishing an idea.

III: RENEWING

"With affluence and power come escalating expectations, and as our level of wealth and comforts keeps increasing, the sense of well-being we hoped to achieve keeps receding into the distance."

- Mihaly Csikszentmihalyi, Flow

17

OPTING OUT

Always know why you are doing what you are doing

Why are you at work today? I don't mean your paycheck work, but your so-called passionate work. For us, work could mean pushing out another product, going to a networking event, or updating your website. Why are you doing it right now? Why are you compelled to produce, to move... to show up?

The question is not as banal as it seems. Mainstream musicians come out with a new album every 18 months, often not because they are inspired like clockwork, but because they (and/or their publishers) are afraid the public will forget their name. Authors churn out books to keep themselves known, too, and even if they currently have a best-seller, they will want to have another one coming as the current one takes its' inevitable fall off the charts. Entrepreneurs fight for success, get that success, and then immediately chase after the next success as they don't want to be viewed as a one-hit wonder.

I can relate to two out of three of these things (hint: I don't play any instruments).

What all three of these examples, and countless other similar scenarios, have in common is fear. We are afraid of losing our place in the world. If we stop, then we will be replaced with a newer, smarter model. We must feed the beast.

It may be the most widely used performance hack. It is also the most short sighted.

It's like performing with a gun to your head: Sure, it gets you motivated to be productive, but at a certain point your body, mind, or soul will give out and you will have to stop, no matter the consequences. That's called burnout. It's called being productive the wrong way.

Instead, you have to listen to, understand by, and give respect to your natural cycle. You will not be productive all the time. You are not meant to be productive all the time. In fact, you are best when you are not productive all the time, as less productive periods give you the opportunity to think, to strategize, and to optimize your energy for the next sprint.

If you want to understand why we often don't respect our own productive cycles, then you have to look at how we view others. As creatives – and entrepreneurs, no matter the ilk, are creatives, too – we face a tremendous amount of pressure to perform. You came up with a brilliant melody? Come up with another one. Can we get another game-changing novel? When are you going to get another startup idea that will shift business forever? We are all guilty of having these expectations, explicitly or implicitly, on the creatives we admire the most. It is why we get desperate, angry, or dismissive at the Salingers of the world: People who produce based on some personal schedule, not on some worldly expectation.

Vulture's Rembert Browne articulated the psychosis well in an article about Andre 3000, Frank Ocean, and other mainstream performers who produce seemingly on their own time:

High quality multi-talents with both infrequent outputs and low profiles make us uncomfortable. We love them, but we're jealous of them, and, possibly, deep down we hate them, because they're doing what we all want to do: Opt out. The way they've decided to live reminds us of how wrong we're all doing it. When people go against the grain of the system, it's a reminder that we're the robots — and the weirdos are the actual humans.

The lessons here are many. First, productivity comes in two forms: Productivity for the public approval and productivity for your passion. It's possible to discover transformative ideas and map out brilliant strategies *without anyone else knowing and with no public proof.* It's OK.

Second, if you produce all the time, then it is easy to lose your voice for the sound of the crowd. The outside voices could be your customers, your family, or your backers. Remember, the people have invested in *your* voice, not the other way around.

No one is going to tell you when it is time to put the tools away and sit down for a second. Only you know when that moment is. And you absolutely always know when that moment is. You just need to be brave enough to listen.

18

LOOKING FOR A CRISIS
Avoid making up things to feel productive

If you are like me, then you get excitement from making difficult situations manageable and impossible scenarios work. Business, and startups specifically, strive on people disrupting monolithic systems and solving long-term problems.

The issue is that the very same bug that gets under our skin to fix things can also make us addicted to the rush of chaos. VC Mark Suster calls it "urgency addiction" and defines it well better than I can:

People with the "urgency addition" thrive on the pressure. We rise to the occasion as it stirs our creative juices. There is something about the adrenaline rush of being under time pressure that excites us and teases out our creativity. We get away with having the urgency addiction because we perform well under pressure. Not everybody does.

The problem, Suster says, is that there a lot of things that are urgent, but few that are important. As he mentions, productivity guru Stephen Covey discussed the idea many years ago in the seminal book *First Things First*.

I have sympathy for Suster and his type of urgency addiction, but I believe it goes a bit deeper than that.

There are two types of urgency addition: personality and environmental.
Suster's great post breaks down what it's like for someone who has a personality leaning towards urgency. As he says, everything is a crisis, and rushing to get things done makes him feel accomplished. More worrisome, he gets a great adrenaline rush from when he finishes things, saving himself from ruin just in the nick of time.

My urgency addiction, however, is different. Throw me on a proverbial desert island and I will be as calm as the breeze. Put me around other people, though, and it can be terribly easy to absorb their attitude - particularly if they are in crisis mode. I'd call this an environmental urgency addiction.

A good personal example for me would be my young family. If you have kids, then you know that minor things to adults are big, imposing things to little ones, which means meltdowns, tears and frustrations. Transpose that energy into a startup (yes, there is a direct parallel between the two experiences) and you can see how a chaotic environment can put me into urgency mode over things that are relatively minor. You are orbiting the giant hairball, as the late Gordon MacKenzie put it, and trying not to get caught in it.

Whether you are a personal or environmental urgency junkie, there are a few survival tactics to keep your head together.

- Remind yourself that it isn't a crisis
- Ask yourself if it will matter 5 minutes, 5 months or 5 years from now
- Forgive yourself for going there

In *The War of Art*, Steven Pressfield found that creatives were more susceptible to "creating soap opera in our lives". However, unlike the amateur, "The working artist will not tolerate trouble in her life because she knows trouble prevents her from doing her work." We need the excitement and the adventure, but it is much easier to make personal drama than it is for us to sit down, shut up, and put that passion into our art.

Think about all the things that feel like a crisis in your life right now, and then how many are real, absolute crisis that have no chance of being resolved on their own. If you channeled that excess anxiety over imagined crisis into your work, then how productive would you be today?

19

LESS, BETTER EMAIL
Do less emails, more actions

Inbox Zero is a great, wonderful goal, where you have no emails sitting in your mailbox. It is also fairly unrealistic for an entrepreneur. How often do you have every deal, relationship and invoice wrapped up like so many loose threads tied into a neat bow? I actually achieved it once recently, and keeping it is a daily battle.

Clearing our inbox may be a Sisyphean affair, but we're ignoring another part of the problem: The length of the messages we get. The longer the email, the longer it often takes to get to the actual action item. And as much as fellow communication specialists decry the shortening of our language in texts, emojis, and, well, Slack, we still manage to write emails the length of newspaper articles.
Can't we just get to the point? Evidently not.

Fast Company's Liz Funk recently ran a good (and short!) piece on the rules to briefer stronger emails. It's worth reading in whole, but I particularly like her best rule:

"2. Never send an email that's more than five sentences long"

That's right. How much more effective would your messaging be if you got straight to the point? It's not a matter of being curt or brisk, but circumventing all the unnecessary fluff that goes into your email discussions.

Sticking to five sentences means you can't acquiesce when it comes to an "ask", nor can you hide in "maybes" when you actually mean "no". Instead, you are forced to be clear, succinct and respectful of everyone's time - including your own.

All of Funk's top three rules are worth considering, too:
1. Take the number of words you think your email should be, cut that number in half, and that's what your word count should be.
2. Never send an email that's more than five sentences long.
3. Put the most important information first.

I'd add a few more rules myself:
4. Consider email part of a bigger conversation, not the whole conversation, so it isn't necessary to put every single detail in one note.
5. Assume the reader does not have much time to pore over your email.
6. If an email is becoming abnormally lengthy, then perhaps email is not the right medium.

Most of all, I appreciate Funk's the simple summary of why you should care:

For solopreneurs, freelancers, and sales professionals who make their living pitching, having a perfectly crafted, short email introduction can drastically increase your success rate. For those making an ask via email, a message that is brief and adds value is more likely to receive a response. For everyone else, sending shorter emails doesn't always take less time, but it does stack the odds in your favor for whatever you aim to accomplish.

Isn't that enough to take the five-sentence challenge? I know it is for me.

20

CREATE "ME" TIME
Even ambitious entrepreneurs can create space for themselves

Entrepreneurship isn't conducive to balanced health, balanced relationships or, really, balanced anything. The rub is that the very vacation, break, or me-time you are postponing could give you the insight you need to move your business forward. We expect to be geniuses at business, but don't give ourselves time to recharge our brains.

I get it: My daily life has been raising my young family, writing and public speaking, and, most recently, leading my startup to acquisition. Here are three ways I keep myself together.

Meditate
Perhaps you, like I once did, think of monk-filled temples or planning to learn it during a trip to the mountains. I view it now as just taking a moment to be fully present in your life: No multitasking, no planning, and no distractions. I rarely get silence, so I will carve out a time daily to sit cross-legged, close my eyes, and breathe in and out. I just do it for a few minutes a day, usually every day. And, as my Buddhist friend A. Raymond Johnson once shared with me, even riding a bike or washing the dishes can be turned into a meditative activity. It is

about stopping, fully taking in your life and enjoying it.

Do one selfish thing

It is crucial to do something daily that has absolutely nothing to do with anyone or anything else. It means it won't grow your business, help your family, or improve your money. If you can carve out time to juggle your business, your personal relationships and other commitments, you can make 10 minutes to do something fun just for you. For me, as a music fan, it might mean taking a random moment in the day to listen to John Coltrane uninterrupted. It is surprisingly refreshing.

Have downtime

As entrepreneurs, we often try to kill two birds with one stone by incorporating our research or work into our downtime: Reading a business book or watching a TED Talk on our business area. I argue that this isn't really downtime, but light work. To mean, downtime means doing something not related to your work at all: It may mean watching a viral video to see what the talk is about, going on a walk in your neighborhood, or spending a few minutes catching up with an old friend.

21

THE WHISKEY METHOD
Look back to go forward

Forgetting the past will not make you more productive. It is a common misconception. Smart planning, excellent ideas, and impressive vision will not help you if you don't possess two traits: Confidence and gratitude. Both reside in your history.

The past reminds you of what you have overcome, which gives you confidence to move forward, and it shows you what you have accomplished, which gives you gratitude for the current moment.

Confidence can be relatively easy to find, but gratitude is a rather slippery one. The most productive people have their own wise method of finding it: *The 4-Hour Work Week* author Tim Ferriss writes briefly in a gratitude journal every morning and night, while media mogul Oprah Winfrey meditates often.

I regularly meditate and occasionally journal, too, but my most effective process is reminding myself where I was a year, five years, or even ten years ago.

I call it the Whiskey Method.

A few years back, the popular scotch whiskey Johnny Walker had a wonderful ad campaign. They would take a popular icon or even an upstart entrepreneur and show their timeline to their modern success. As a made-up example, "1966 Backup Guitarist, 1967 Debut Album, 1969 Rock Legend" would be for Jimi Hendrix. It would end with a simple motto: "Keep walking".

The problem is that we tend to lionize people, particularly ourselves, *after* they've made it. We often don't define what "making it" means, nor do we celebrate the many, many victories it takes to even get there. We don't respect the journey. And, as writers more thoughtful than I have said, you can't expect to be given more if you don't appreciate what you already have. Why would your so-called muse deliver more creativity and insight when you didn't give her props for helping you in the past? The Whiskey Method is that gratitude.

Here is mine:
- 2005 Published First Book
- 2010 Published First Best-seller
- 2013 Started First Startup
- 2014 Did First TED Talk
- 2015 Sold Second Startup

It is both inspiring and humbling to me that I just began writing books about a decade ago, and you are now reading my 18th one. It is even more beautiful that I started my entrepreneurial journey only three years ago, yet have had enough adventures to share with others. I immediately feel like forgiving myself for the mistakes I've made this month, this week, or even this day.

The frustrations, setback, and challenges in my day-to-day grind begin to fall away, as I realize not that much time has passed. I am still a student. And now, as I realize how quickly I've transformed as a person, I start to respect the progress I make today – and that means I'll be more productive than I would have been otherwise.

22

SILENCE IS GOLDEN
Periodically shut up to make progress

It's always more comfortable to take action. It is the negotiator who can't handle the uncomfortable lull in the conversation, the artist who keeps fiddling with her finished work or the child who has to do what he was just told not to do. The absence of something is always more frightening than having undesired results from our actions.

If we embraced silence as part of the natural ebb and flow of our lives, then we would be stronger, smarter, and savvier when it is actually time to take action. Meditation, yoga and other practices can help get your mind into a clearer space.

You can also just stop talking.

A recent Duke University study found that quiet actually improves memory and awareness, per *Nautilus Magazine*:

Kirste found that two hours of silence per day prompted cell development in the hippocampus, the brain region related to the formation of memory, involving the senses. This was deeply puzzling: The total absence of input was having a more pronounced effect than any sort of input tested.

152

Here's how Kirste made sense of the results. She knew that "environmental enrichment," like the introduction of toys or fellow mice, encouraged the development of neurons because they challenged the brains of mice. Perhaps the total absence of sound may have been so artificial, she reasoned--so alarming, even--that it prompted a higher level of sensitivity or alertness in the mice.

Like taking a short nap or planning a blank day, creating quiet time is a conscious act towards productivity disguised as a leisure activity. We schedule power meetings, brainstorms, hackathons, and vacations. Why aren't we scheduling silence? It is worth blocking off a daily hour of quiet - not inactivity, but silence - and seeing how it changes your productivity.

23

BULLETPROOF

The more you know yourself, the more space you have to be productive

Pressure to be productive can actually stress us out to the point where we are no longer potent, and it usually comes from two places: internal and external. The internal pressure reminds you that there is a particular, often idealized goal you planned to reach and you will absolutely not reach it if you do not hit a certain level of productivity. The external pressure tells you that other people will judge you or, worse, stop you from reaching the goal if you aren't being productive fast enough.

The internal pressure can be relieved by setting realistic milestones, creating limitations to encourage focus, and maintaining your self-care. The external pressure is much more nefarious. It is the competitor that you know now, or perhaps the unknown competitor in the near future that can snuff you out at any time. It is the loved one that, whether he said anything or not, you know is just waiting for you to fail so he can be proven right. It is the loyal customers who you think will be disappointed if you do not deliver as quickly as you would like. It is the invisible "they". And, to use a popular sports saying, "They cannot be stopped, only contained."

Containing the external pressure can be done in one simple way: Understand what you are not. By knowing what you are not, you have little to worry about with other people derailing or duplicating your success. A good example is the ride-sharing services Lyft and Uber. On paper, they sound like similar companies, both employing everyday drivers to turn their own vehicles into ad hoc taxis. The identities couldn't be more different, though: Uber pushes the remote, cool personal limo feel, as it originally only utilized black cars, while Lyft represents the fun, collegiate experience, with its cars initially having big pink moustaches stuck on their bumpers. Talk about branding! I know many creatives that hate the word "branding", but that's what you are doing when you say you only work with small organizations, or your boutique caters to the working class, or your startup was created for hungry millennials, and so on. It is what separates *you* from *them*. And separating yourself is a hell of a lot easier when it comes from your own identity, as you don't have to work so hard to be authentic. I heard Uber co-founder Travis Kalanick speak at TED and there is no way you could see him and believe he created Lyft. The Uber brand is a representation of him, through and through. You nor I could recreate Uber, even with a billion dollars. Uber belongs only to Travis. People can compete, but they cannot replicate.

Identifying what you are not, and therefore quieting the external pressure, is important for two reasons. First, putting the focus on proving something to the outside world is a ridiculous task: If you are doing anything worthwhile, then there will be critics, and those critics will never be silenced. It is a waste of precious time. Second, worrying about the external pressure will take you out of your own natural productive cycle. Get in the wrong headspace and you could be shipping products to please the public when your work actually needed more time to gestate, or taking on more duties to hush critics when you should be better managing your tasks at hand. Again, you have an instinct for when you should be pursuing, when you should be doing, and when you should be renewing. Not having a rock-solid identity could have you dramatically trying to force productivity based on the fickle public.

Master marketer Seth Godin explains it further:

"At some point, you need to decide who you are. You need to understand the scale of what you built. You need to decide what the brand is when people hire you and when they engage with you... [and] we can't jump to the next thing instantly nor can we complain that picking one scale keeps us from doing the other thing. We have to embrace it. The fact is that it helps us that we have a sinecure, that we have a niche, that we have a thing that we do, 'cuz then, when other people want to be in our

space just for kicks, they can't! They are not us at our scale with our contribution to make."

The more you clarify what you are not, the more bulletproof you become. Then you can take your time, follow your own productivity cycle, and push away worries about being replaced – because you can't be.

24
SHADOWBOXING
Fact: Most of your fears will not come to pass

Entrepreneurship is all about anticipation. You have to know what the market wants before you deliver or, when it comes to the financial end, what the markets will bear before you price your product. You have to guess what your competition is going to do when you launch your service. You have to be ready for when your idea goes viral because, as argued in THE BITE-SIZED ENTREPRENEUR, you have to prepare for success as much as you do for failure. And why, again, are we more prone to anxiety and sleepless nights? Honestly, it could be a chicken and egg paradox, as entrepreneurial personalities tend to be focused on the future anyway.

The question is, what do you do with all that nervousness about tomorrow?

Nothing.

Recognize it, sit with it, accept it, and let it leave.

The spiritual writer Pema Chodron has a great analogy for us. It is unedited and shown at length for full effect:

There's a Zen story in which a man is enjoying himself on a river at dusk. He sees another boat coming down the river toward him. At first it seems so nice to him that someone else is also enjoying the river on a nice summer evening. Then he realized that the boat is coming right toward him, faster and faster. He begins to yell, "Hey, hey, watch out! For Pete's sake, turn aside!" But the boat just comes right at him, faster and faster. By this time he's standing up in his boat, screaming and shaking his fist, and then the boat smashes right into him. He sees that it's an empty boat.

I laughed out loud when I first read this story more than a decade ago. I laughed again when I stumbled upon the story again this past week, the same week where I swung my fist angrily at many empty boats. Some situations, I believe, I actually made worse because of my reactions. In fact, they weren't even actual situations *until* I reacted! As a comedian once said, I could kick my own ass.

Before beating myself up about it, though, I paused and realized that this is all part of our process. We are always surrounded by empty boats careening at reckless speeds into our emotional, mental, and professional lives, and, frankly, for many of us, those three lives are all the same. It becomes about reacting to things that are real, not to things that make us feel a certain way. It is separating our facts from our fears. It is about accepting our anxiousness for the future and understanding that it has absolutely nothing to do with what will happen in next minute. Because we don't know that.

Be thankful for your empty boats, as they carry one of the most valuable insights: your personal fear. My boat is different than your boat. The boat represents your issues, your scars, your past. It is entirely possible to live your life swinging at shadows, taking actions based on some vague anxiety about the future. Many people spend years fighting for security – no matter what the price. When you step into entrepreneurship, though, you have to understand why you are driven and what motivates you. It is the key to success, as someone who doesn't know why they are getting up in the morning, sacrificing their time, and risking their livelihood for something will not be an entrepreneur for very long. Others may have the luxury of clinging to routine, repetition, and stability to keep their fears at bay. We do not have that option.

As a result, the moments where we can see, feel, and identify our fears are truly gifts to our future selves.

"Fear is often an indicator that you're going in the right direction," *Unmistakable* author Srinivas Rao puts it. "It repeatedly indicates your next new level."

Do you know what you are afraid of now? Congratulations. Now you know your pain point, the area where you need to grow, and that knowledge will get you a step closer to mastering yourself. It is an insight people who never take the entrepreneurial journey will rarely understand.

ON BALANCING
(THE BALANCED BITE-SIZED ENTREPRENEUR)

To Parul,
my partner on this wild, wonderful journey.
Thank you.

WHY THIS BOOK SHOULDN'T EXIST

This book almost didn't happen. The first Bite-Sized Entrepreneur book came quickly, as did The Productive Bite-Sized Entrepreneur. I had just sold my startup, Cuddlr, after an 11-month run as co-founder, and spent a year writing about my experiences for Inc. Magazine, specifically leading a high-profile startup while being a fully-present, hands-on stay-at-home dad of a baby. There was a lot to say! Fresh from Silicon Valley, the belief was that you could not succeed as an entrepreneur and maintain a romantic partnership, nevertheless a family. I wanted to show people that it was possible.

And then, suddenly, I was done.

The first book rocketed up to the top of the Amazon Entrepreneurship books, with the second one following behind, and I began juggling media interviews and requests along with the writing, the consulting and the entrepreneurial advising – you know, how I actually made a living. And I'm still a stay-at-home dad with a new toddler and, now, another son.

I had to make a choice: Focus on the goal of completing the trilogy or admit that the goal didn't fit my new world. So, I'm going to kill myself to write THE BALANCED BITE-SIZED ENTREPRENEUR?

"How absurd", I told my closest confidantes, "for me to burn myself out writing a book about creating balance."

So, I stopped.

In retrospect, it wasn't a stop, but rather a thoughtful pause. Much has happened in the year since the last Bite-Sized Entrepreneur, but most of it was internal. I learned how to be fully present for two kids, pay more attention to my body (the first books talked about me waking up at 3:15 am to lead my company – and the aftermath), and become grateful for the bit of wisdom I was able to share already in the best-selling books.

More importantly, I began listening to you. I lean towards strategy, so I had all the books planned out, from general launch dates to major discussion points. What I didn't realize until my pause is that you, not me, would tell me what you need. *You tell me how I can best serve you.*

I traveled the world speaking about the Bite-Sized Entrepreneur methods, from Durham, NC, to Bogota, Colombia, to my previous hometown of San Diego. What's amazing was that I'd get the same two questions:

"Do I have enough to start?" and "Do I have enough to keep going?"

I always respond to the first question quickly, drawing in the topics of starting small, ideally as a side hustle, and organizing your life based on priorities, to maximize productivity. It's the first two books! Maintaining, though, was what you really needed. Sure, you can get started and have your prioritizes in order, but if your mind isn't in some sense of balance, then all the resources, time, or passion in the world won't bring you to your definition of success.

Therefore, THE BALANCED BITE-SIZED ENTREPRENEUR goes deeper. How do you manage within chaos? How do you know what to focus on? How do you know when to quit? There are no easy answers, nor should there be. If you haven't already, read through the first two books, particularly The Bite-Sized Entrepreneur, to build a strong foundation for the concepts addressed here. You should know why persistence always trumps patience and why "No" is the absolute best word for your growth.

And, after reading this book, you'll have a better sense of how to maintain that beautiful structure and mindset you established based on the first two in the trilogy. This third book wouldn't have been possible without me spending a year growing enough to write it. I hope it was worth the wait for you. It was for me.

-Damon Brown, October 2017

I: LET GO

"All spiritual traditions emphasize the need to keep you attention in the present time. As long as you remain present, everything you need is present with you."

-Caroline Myss, Sacred Contracts

1
THE 3-MINUTE RULE
A few focused minutes will change your entire day

Our attention spans are arguably getting shorter, but our need for depth is getting heavier. It does not feel like enough to commit a little or to make small edits. Today, we have romanticized the broad stroke, the sweeping changes, and the dramatic declaration. Perhaps it isn't that our attention spans are shorter, but rather that a remarkable amount of things are clamoring for our attention, and that, to paraphrase both futurist Jared Lanier and iconic entrepreneur Seth Godin, is too much for our lizard brains to handle.

In other words, we feel like we have to make dramatic shifts to make any type of long-lasting impact on our lives.

The good news is that we can push slowly and confidently to our goals. We can take little steps, so small that they're almost unperceivable in our daily lives, and significantly change our insight, our strength, and our overall viewpoint.

Here's what you can do in three minutes a day.

Meditation

173

It started when I moved to New Orleans. I felt like I need to get quiet, not on the outside (NoLa is never a quiet place!), but on the inside. So I sat in my little bed, crossed my legs, and just closed my eyes. I repeated the same thing nearly every day since 2004.

The catch is that my practice is three minutes. I'll occasionally do five minutes on rough days, when I feel like I can't sit still, or on great days, when I actually crave the silence it provides. Just recently, I tried doing twice a day: Midmorning, after I get our youngest son down for his first nap, and mid-evening, after I get our youngest down for his sleep.

The key is that it is so tiny that it has stayed with me, from being a young man escaping Hurricane Katrina to a full-time journalist living in downtown San Francisco to a new entrepreneur (and dad) in San Diego to, now, as a veteran stay-at-home dad and consultant in Toledo, Ohio. I can *always* spare three minutes to sit. You can, too.

Goal setting

Poker champion Phil Hellmuth wrote his six major life goals on a piece of paper and put it on his bathroom mirror (he hit five out of six within a few years, including winning the World Series of Poker). Entrepreneur Elon Musk put his goal for the electric car on a random Tumblr blog and, ten years later, Tesla was the leader in the vehicle

174

space.

I write down my goals on index cards, sometimes once a quarter, sometimes once a year, often with a deadline. It takes three minutes. In 2014, I did a TED talk about the power of index cards, which was nine minutes longer than the time I take to write down my ideas. Chances are you already know what you want. Write it down. It won't take long.

A few things happen when you put it down on paper. First, you are forced to articulate your vision, which makes it more concrete than something floating in your mind. Second, you've got a compass to guide all your decisions. Got a new opportunity? If it doesn't fit into your ultimate goals, then it can (and should) be a quick "No". Third, as the late motivational speaker Jim Rohn said, you can actually keep track of your growth. What were your goals a year ago? If you don't know, then you can't see – and celebrate – how much you've grown.

Again, three minutes of your time.

Enjoy your environment
Consider the world your playground. For me, it hit me when we had our first kid, and those daily miles-long walks I took to clear my mind were unrealistic. Instead, my exercise and motion had to

175

come from pacing carrying my son, walking while I was on the phone, or, later, pushing his stroller up and down San Diego hills.

What I began to do is savor opportunities to move more. I'd travel through airports and take the stairs rather than the escalator. Later, when I'd have the time during layovers, I'd skip the people mover and even the trains to briskly walk to the next terminal. These bite-sized improvements led to me being in some of the best shape of my life, despite the natural chaos of running an ambitious home career with two young kids.

For you, it could be parking a little further from the grocery store, skipping the elevator in two story buildings, or other small changes.

Consistent action, not dramatic action, fuels growth.

2
PUT YOUR MASK ON FIRST
Assume tomorrow won't provide your rest

There's a reason we are comfortable sacrificing it all to make our businesses a reality: We assume we'll get a break tomorrow. To paraphrase Orphan Annie, tomorrow is always a day away--but meanwhile we could end up being useless to the very people we say we are sacrificing everything for.

Consultant Alan Weiss calls this the Oxygen Mask Principle. If you're in an emergency situation on an airplane, you are told to put your oxygen mask on first before assisting a less competent companion. He breaks it down in his podcast, The Way I See It:

You can't help the client or your family, you can't do pro bono work, you can't help others in the profession, you can't help anyone unless you yourself are comfortable. You need a healthy selfishness.

Weiss wrote *Value-Based Fees*, one of my favorite business books, and it is refreshing to hear such a driven businessman discuss the need for balance. As I talked about in *The Productive Bite-Sized Entrepreneur*, being busy does not equal productivity--and continuous exhaustion will not only make your work sloppy but ultimately wreck both you and your business.

Ironically, prioritizing your self-care is the best way to take care of others. How are you taking care of yourself today?

3

YOU NEED LONGER DEADLINES
Unnecessary pressure often creates disappointing results

It is Monday morning and I've already had a failure this week. I have a product I worked hard to finish and roll out today, but the pieces didn't come together on time. It was sometime mid-Sunday, shortly after lunch that I realized I'd have to suck it up and let it go.

What is fascinating is that there was no reason for my new product to launch today. No one, aside from a couple confidants, knew it was going to launch. In fact, my work would probably go on fine without it. Coincidentally, just a few weeks ago, someone in my brain trust suggested I try to let go of "false deadlines".

A false deadline is a hard stop you give yourself for some nonconsequential reason. It could be to placate your ego, it could be you want to get a project off your plate, it could be you're just sick of looking at it on the to-do list. The fact is that it actually doesn't matter: You have no external pressure to perform. It is all internal.

Can you relate? Here's how I calm myself down when I see myself setting up (and failing) a false deadline.

Where did this deadline come from?
If you pause for a second, then you may find the origin of your deadline isn't even relevant anymore. I've worked on projects where the aggressive timeline was based on another department's needs - yet when the other group pushed its timeline out, we didn't change ours! The result was us rushing around for quite literally nothing.

When did this deadline become a priority?
I'm a big advocate for not waiting until tomorrow to create the life you want, but it is just as important to know today what moves are *ideal* and what moves are *necessary*. An ideal goal can sneak into the necessary goal category and, suddenly, the amount of pressure you give yourself to reach this ambitious end is significantly higher. I help others be productive and I still struggle with this phenomenon.

What will happen if you don't meet this goal?
This last point is critical, as you have to be able to identify what you fear will happen if you don't meet this false deadline. You can't process the anxiety around meeting the deadline if you don't know what, exactly, you are feeling.

For me, I'm proud of what I've created, so missing today's deadline means I have to wait longer to share it. Disappointing? Definitely. Career threatening? Far from it. And oftentimes, when I have missed a false deadline, opportunities to make the product greater have popped up after the fact - making the temporary pain all the more worthwhile. It's just a matter of remember this *while* it is happening.

4
CHECK THE WEATHER FIRST
Even the best effort is a waste when the timing is wrong

Life is probably significantly different for you now than it was five years, one year, or maybe even one month ago. The sentiment is strong for me, especially in the wake of a cross-country move, but there are other reasons why I've been thinking about change lately. Being back in the Midwest, where I had my teenage years, means trading a decade of neutral West Coast seasons for the gorgeous, crisp turning of the leaves. Winter actually feels intimidating now, but not because I'm afraid of the cold (my biggest TED Talk was in wintery Whistler, British Columbia, Canada). Rather, the prospect of shorter days and frigid nights makes me feel closer to nature, as if, post-California, I am suddenly exposed after being sheltered away from the rest of the world.

It feels invigorating to follow the flow of the seasons and actually, consciously, let things naturally whither away. There are ideas that later became principles and passions that became dogma. The pursuit of a big, hairy, ambitious goal became the focus rather than remembering why I created the goal in the first place. For many reasons, big goals that I set for myself as recently as a year ago now seem almost silly. Contrary to common belief, it is not easier to give up. It is actually easier to keep fighting, as at least you feel like you're making progress.

When you pause, though, you can see how ridiculous it feels planting a tomato seed during an ice storm or crossing a raging river when it isn't anywhere near frozen. It's just that, before the quiet moment, you aren't paying attention to the natural flow of your world. You're just trying to reach your goal.

The near-misses, almost-wases, and should-have-beens have been plentiful lately and, frankly, feel more robust than they've been in my life in a long while. So do the coincidences and absolutes, as if fate stepped in and said 'Nah, you're going that way. I'll make sure of that!' It pleases my ego to say that I am one determined individual, which is why life has to react so forcefully when I should be going in a different direction. And, as the world slows down and I slowly get over myself, I am becoming amazed at how, to paraphrase Steve Jobs, seemingly random dots of events begin to make a pattern.

But you can only see the evidence when you're looking back. Going forward requires trusting that fall will follow summer. And it always does.

5

FAILURE IS SUCCESS

Holding your nose during a failure misses the point

Failure is a prerequisite for getting what you want, and often it puts us in the direction to get what we actually need. It gave Apple's Steve Jobs a mission, Shark Tank's Daymond John a vision, and every entrepreneur you know a groundedness not achievable otherwise. To paraphrase Brené Brown, the only guarantee you have when you step in the arena is that you will get your butt kicked.

So when one of the most successful women in the world talks about her failures, it is wise to listen.

In 1998, Oprah Winfrey's big-budget movie *Beloved* was set to be her splash into Hollywood. Her agent called her the day after opening night and told her it was already a flop. She was devastated.

Two decades later, she is even more powerful than before. How does that happen? There are three telling quotes:

Gratitude
"That's when the gratitude practice became really strong for me, because it's hard to remain sad if

you're focused on what you have instead of what you don't have."

There are volumes of anecdotal and scientific evidence showing that gratitude for what you currently have leads to your getting more of what you want. Your brain focuses on what you focus on, so concentrating on what's missing will only show you what you lack, not the new opportunities available.

Service

"It taught me to never again--never again, ever--put all of your hopes, expectations, eggs in the basket of box office. Do the work as an offering, and then whatever happens, happens."

Your job is to create something that the world needs -- and that's it. Profitability comes from prioritizing your employees and your customers, not from prioritizing profitability. Market share comes from creating a service of value, not from focusing on market share. In Oprah's case, she gives and gives, and her customers choose to give their financial, emotional, and mental support in return.

Presence

"There's not a human being alive who doesn't want--in any conversation, encounter, experience with another human being--to feel like they matter.

And you can resolve any issue if you could just get to what it is that they want--they want to be heard. And they want to know that what they said to you meant something. Most people go their entire lives and nobody ever really wants the answer to 'How are you? Tell me about yourself.'"

It is ridiculously easy to depersonalize people because of your goals: networking with someone just to get something out of it, manipulating customers to reach a new milestone, or simply not taking the time to take care of the people who gave you success in the first place.

Gratitude, service, and presence can bring you to your goals -- and help you overcome the many failures it will take to get there.

6

DO GOOD ENOUGH
Perfection prevents greatness

We have a cultural obsession with extreme experiences: Things have to be uber or incredible or outstanding or breathtaking. The obsession pours into our expectations of ourselves, as it isn't enough to get funding, but to be a unicorn, and being a simple company is inadequate compared to being a grand disrupter.

It also means we tend to kill our ideas, if not our own success, before they have a chance to be great.

In praise of good enough

The best thing you can do is go for good. It doesn't mean settling for good when great is available. It means understanding that good is actually good, and that everything you do is intended as a start, not as a permanent state.

Ironically, while Silicon Valley is focused on "crushing it", the popular Lean Startup model is based on the very idea of good enough. In short, you take your idea, create it with as little resources as possible and get your good enough take - your minimal viable product - to your intended audience as quickly as possible.

The problem with high expectations

The feedback from your audience takes your idea from good to great. High expectations alone won't get you there. In fact, high expectations are likely to hamper your progress.

Ryan Holiday and Stephen Hanselman's *The Daily Stoic* explains that most of our frustration isn't with our progress, but with our expectations. We could have extraordinary success yet, if we are expecting an unrealistic amount of progress, that rare success won't even feel like an accomplishment.

The success trap
An excellent cautionary tale is iconic performer Michael Jackson handling the success of his breakthrough album *Thriller*. The late icon worked with megaproducer Quincy Jones and essentially redefined R & B - *Thriller* is still one of the top 20 selling albums of all time. The problem? Jackson wanted to do it again. According to Jones, he spent the rest of his life, album after album, trying to create something bigger than Thriller. As a result, he never felt quite satisfied.

Keep in mind, Jones wasn't saying something equal to *Thriller*. Something more successful than *Thriller*. One of the best-selling albums of all time.

The Atlantic explained the challenge during the 25th anniversary of *Bad*, the critically-panned *Thriller* follow-up:

188

Jackson in interviews more often expressed Olympian commercial goals of breaking the sales records of his previous album than he did of pursuing new musical territory. And very much like how many filmmakers of blockbusters beef up defining fight scenes and plotlines, Jackson conspicuously restaged and amplified Thriller's signature moments with perfectionist's precision, making Bad sound sterile in too many places.

It is an amazing trap: You naturally hit a home run and, next time up to bat, you're checking wind conditions, wearing a lucky hat and trying to recreate the previous experience.

The rub is that what you did - the success you had - wasn't just based on your actions. It is both timing and inspiration, too. The sales success of *Thriller* could not be recreated because the whole record industry sold less records, as we would see with Napster and iTunes and Spotify. The needs of the listeners changed (ironically, because of *Thriller* itself), so doing another *Thriller* wouldn't recreate the same sea change. And Jackson was arguably in a different place, as he now had ridiculously high expectations of himself and a new set of pressures.

Lightning won't strike in the same place twice
Sometimes we expect to do the same amazing work twice, so we get sloppy the second time around. Just as often, though, we can give ourselves too

much credit for our success, overanalyzing what we did initially as if our win was completely based on our actions.

It is wiser to be humble and focused rather than just expecting an unlikely win. And in a true Zen way, setting smaller, realistic goals leads us bigger long-term success.

7

MAKE YOUR SACRIFICE WORTH IT
Know when you're going to quit ahead of time

We have a cultural obsession with extreme experiences: Things have to be uber or incredible or outstanding or breathtaking. The obsession pours into our expectations of ourselves, as it isn't enough to get funding, but to be a unicorn, and being a simple company is inadequate compared to being a grand disrupter.

It also means we tend to kill our ideas, if not our own success, before they have a chance to be great.

Quitting is severely underrated. If you've been following entrepreneurial leadership, then you know that everyone from Steve Jobs to the Google founders built their success on quitting. So why are we obsessed with making things work instead of just accepting that some of our ideas have run their course?

On its decade anniversary, it is worth taking another read of business maverick Seth Godin's classic *The Dip: A Little Book That Teaches You When to Quit (And When to Stick)*. I just rediscovered *The Dip* on audiobook, and perhaps the biggest insight we can all use is this:

Write down under what circumstances you're willing to quit.

To explain, Godin quotes ultramarathoner Dick Collins: "Decide before the race the conditions that will cause you to decide to stop and drop out. You don't want to be out there saying, 'Well, gee, my leg hurts, I'm a little dehydrated, I'm sleepy, I'm tired, and it's cold, and it's windy...' and talk yourself into quitting."

If you're making a decision based on how you're feeling at that moment, then you will probably make the wrong decision.

You don't quit when the going gets rough. You quit when you know you've invested more than you'll get out of it. You need clear, measurable metrics to know when to give up on your big idea or business.

Here are a few I've recently used:

I'll spend this much money
I self-financed *The Bite-Sized Entrepreneur: 21 Ways to Ignite Your Passion and Pursue Your Side Hustle.* I set a budget and a timeline to recoup that money. It hit the Amazon Entrepreneur book Top 10, which helped me reach the goal and do a follow-up book, *The Productive Bite-Sized Entrepreneur: 24 Smart Secrets to Do More in Less Time.* If I didn't

recoup, then there would be no follow up – and you wouldn't be reading this book right now!

I'll spend this much time
I spent a good amount of time on a side hustle and gave myself a few months to make it work. And, with no fanfare, I recently shut it down. Why? Come to find out, no one wanted it. To paraphrase Godin, the temporary pain of giving up is better than the slow death of mindlessly continuing.

I'll spend this much effort
I love working on new ideas, and there is one that I had been toiling away on for years. Within the last few days, I realized that the effort is too great to make it real based on my current time, priorities and resources. It sucks, but moving forward with it begs the question: How much of my life would I have to upheaval to make this thing a reality and, if I see myself at the finish line, would it have been worth it?

Give yourself permission to say, "No, it isn't worth it." And give yourself permission *before* you actually start.

8

THE ULTIMATE TIME LIMIT
Always remember your time can end at any moment

There is a simple reason why we procrastinate: We assume we will have more time. There is more time to make it perfect, more time to connect with others and more time to pursue that brilliant idea. But success lies in knowing that time will run out - and that we will die.

In two decades, successful entrepreneur Ricardo Semler turned Semco Partners from a four million dollar company to a 212 million-dollar company - namely by creating an intuitive, innovative work environment, shared in his best-selling book *Maverick*. Semler is also a very happy man, but he says it has nothing to do with his financial or business success. As he recently explained to Tim Ferriss, Semler's real secret is treating each day as his last.

I kept thinking 'Geez, I don't want to be in that situation where suddenly now I have to go to ballgames with the kids and I have to travel to places I haven't been and I have to write that play that I never wrote.' That's crazy. Let's do something else... So, on Mondays and Thursdays I have what I call 'Terminal Days', the two days a week in which my schedule is completely clear and I do on those days what I would have done if I heard this conversation from my oncologist.

This habit isn't just for show. Semler says melanoma runs in his family, so most of his relatives have had a sudden death. He himself has had multiple cancer surgeries that, fortunately, caught the melanoma before it spread. Even though he is 57, Semler faces his own death every day.

Semler sets aside two days a week to do exactly what he would do if it were the last day of his life. It is easy to assume that his work would suffer, but, in fact, he is regularly setting himself up for career greatness. Think about it: If you actually carved out time for personal fulfillment every single week, imagine how focused and productive you would be during the remaining days?

For the ambitious among us, our problem isn't saying "Yes" (as Shonda Rhimes said in her TED Talk), but in saying "No". You have to close a number of doors to truly do what you desire - and material or worldly success only increases the choices over time, making the process even more difficult.

Start making tough decisions now before they get tougher over time. What should you be focusing on today?

9

THE BIGGEST CHANGES
*Like icebergs, most of our growth happens
below the surface*

It has been a summer of transitions for most people
I know, myself included. My family and I recently
moved to the Midwest after spending a dozen
years on the West Coast. I'm fortunate that my
focus, on helping potential and current
entrepreneurs reach their best without burning
themselves out, only gets richer as I connect with
new communities in the Toledo/Detroit area.

Any transition takes a great deal of energy, no
matter how advantageous or exciting it may be. It
is like what writer Elizabeth Gilbert said in one of
my favorite talks I've ever seen at TED: Her
stratospheric success with *Eat, Pray, Love* caused
the same performance anxiety as when she was a
waitressing wannabe writer collecting hundreds of
publishing rejection letters. Both felt like a foreign
place. Her way back to sanity? She started writing
the next thing. She did the work.

The key during transitions isn't just to keep your
focus, but to realize that it will take you more
energy to do so. Like moving to a new town,
previously unconscious acts like going to the
grocery store or remembering a neighbor's name

now require thought, rigor, and presence. You are building the foundation for your next chapter. Most importantly, you are given the opportunity to think about the things you previously assumed to be true and can make a structure better for you today.

All this takes time, all this takes energy, and all this takes patience. So, I'm allowing myself a few extra minutes of meditation each day, an additional breath or two before returning an urgent phone call, and considerable thoughtfulness in my workday strategy. The best gift you can give yourself is the space to get the inner work done to make a stronger you - even if you are the only one who can feel it. You are doing more work than you think.

II: TAKE IN

"For every single thing you want in life, there's a price; a price that has to be paid. And nature always demands that the price be paid in advance."

-Brian Tracy, How to Start and Succeed in Your Own Business

10

EVERY SINGLE DAY
Habits become your life

It's been proven that rituals and habits are the key to success. I meditate nearly every morning. I listen to something thoughtful daily, most recently *The Daily Stoic*. I always walk as much as possible. Still, the rapid evolution of my career gives me days where I question the very point of having these routines. I'm still struggling.

If you can relate, then it is key to remind yourself that practices are the foundation for those very times when you feel like things are going out of control. It is the structure upon which your stability sits.

I often think of an old *SPIN* magazine article featuring River Cuomo, the self-described temperamental leader of the alternative band Weezer. The feature talked about Cuomo taking up meditation, going deep into self discovery and so on. When asked about how he changed, a band member captured the general sentiment well. To paraphrase:

He's still a [explicative]. But imagine how much of a bigger [explicative] he'd be without doing this?

It's not that waking up early, always making your bed or writing down your gratitude will make you transcend disappointment, heartache and failure. It's that your routines will make you more *resilient* to face those obstacles. And, over time, it makes a cumulative effect on your life, like compound interest in the bank.

Pause before you consider subtracting habits out of your life because the results seem invisible. Instead, they could be keeping you afloat and keeping you from going further off your course.

11

CARRY ONE THING AT A TIME
Guilt over focusing on one thing will make you useless at all things

I remember the moment I realized it wasn't going to work. I was in New York, visiting to support a local TED conference, and it hit me that I would not be able to fulfill my new desire: Becoming a worldwide public speaker. My newborn son was at home, along with my toddler, and we crammed together a patchwork of support to cover my absence as the primary caregiver. It required a redeye to even get my day in Manhattan. I'd be flying home that same night, hopefully getting some shuteye at the airport while I waited to board. My boys needed me. My heart needed to be on the road.

Before I left, I had a tea with my friend and mentor, artist Leida Snow. I talked about my ambitions, my opportunities, and my conflict. She smiled, and talked for a bit. This is what I understood:

Balance isn't doing everything at once. Balance is doing what is most important at the time. Sometimes you'll be super present as a dad. Sometimes you'll be super present as an international speaker. It's OK to put one down and pick the other one up. But you can't be both at the same moment.

It reminds me of Buddhist monk Thich Nhat Hanh, whom often talks about anticipation and anxiety for the future (which is the same thing) robbing the pleasure out of an experience when it actually does happen. Or my own research for my book *Our Virtual Shadow: Why We Are Obsessed with Documenting Our Lives Online*, where we pull ourselves out of the moment to capture the moment and, in a sense, don't experience the moment at all.

Bifurcating myself would make me a bad father and a bad public speaker, as I wouldn't be fully invested in either. Instead, when I was at home, my family would have my love and attention, and when I hit the stage, my audience would have me totally engaged in the conversation. It honors me, it honors you, and it honors my family.

Or, as Hanh puts it, "Do one thing at a time. Do it deeply."

12

BUILD LIKE YOU'RE ALREADY THERE
Focus on the small and the big will handle itself

The late, powerful speaker Jim Rohn helped guide Tony Robbins' early career and, as you can imagine, was a force into himself. A quote from one of Rohn's classic talks is still relevant, if not more so today:

"You say, 'If I had a big organization, you know, I'd really run it with a strong hand and I'd be a fabulous leader. But I've only got a few (followers) and I don't know where they are.' See, that's not going to work. If you wish to preside over a lot... you have to be disciplined when the amounts are small."

What Rohn is talking about is *systems*: A system to master your emotional intelligence so you can handle the power; a system to handle your relationships so your management can scale; and a system to organize your resources so you can use them most effectively in high numbers.

The thing is that those systems can most easily be put into place when the overhead is as low as the stakes. Ironically, as Rohn mentions, it's easy to not take the systems seriously when the rewards are weak, yet this is the very time you should be thinking about long-range goals.

It's kind of like wishing to win the lottery, but not actually thinking about what you would do with the money: The chances of you wasting the money if you got it are extremely high. And even if you did have a plan, if you didn't manage things well on the small scale, you certainly wouldn't have the discipline to do it with millions!

Entrepreneurs often learn this the hard way. How many companies end up growing faster than expected, becoming worth billions in a few short years, only to do expensive fixes because they didn't take the time to consider details that felt virtually inconsequential when they were small?

Instead, take a step today - even a small one - to put a system in place so you will be able to better emotionally, relationally and financially handle your business if and when it does reach new heights. It is often more dangerous to prepare for failure than it is for success.

13

THE 20/20 TECHNIQUE
Make the most of your time and of others

The further you get in your field, the more thoughtful you have to be about the time you spend. It often means saying "No" more than you would like. Former Googler Jenny Blake, author of the best-selling book *Pivot*, has a great way to defend your time and help other people.

When someone asks for a brain picking session, Blake instead suggests they do a 20/20 meeting (I interpreted it as 20/20, but the numbers can be higher or lower). The meeting is 20 minutes talking about what you care about and then 20 minutes talking about what the other person cares about.

I love this method for many reasons:

Eliminate the one-way conversation
Blake has a best-selling book, a significant career at the most envied startup in the world and a reputation for helping people get their businesses to the next level. You have your own expertise, too, and it would be too easy for you to give and not receive, especially as you gain prominence in your field. By splitting the time evenly, you remove potential one-sidedness.

Prevent takers from monopolizing time

There are many reasons why people may feel comfortable monopolizing your time, from feeling like you owe them to listen to being just thoughtless about your other obligations. By declaring a split meeting, you create equal expectations from the outset and make it clear that you expect to be receiving value from the meeting, too. Their reaction to your suggestion makes their intentions clearer and can help you decide whether you want to actually spend more time with the person.

Smooth out the power dynamics

Everyone you meet has a piece of insight that can help you or has access to people or social circles that can be beneficial to your business. How do you know if you're the only one giving insight? Instead, the 20/20 rule gives you and your companion equal footing, potentially staving off weird power dynamics and giving both of you an opportunity for growth. And after the meeting, they don't owe you anything, just as you don't owe them anything either.

14

THEORY IS JUST THAT
Don't mistake an idea for a solution

You'd be forgiven for not immediately associating former heavyweight boxing champion Mike Tyson with emotional intelligence, especially if, like me, you remember his more ferocious years. However, he's always had a strong sensitivity and insight under the tough veneer, as shown in documentaries like *Tyson*.

He also has one of the wisest quotes you'll ever hear on how to make emotionally intelligent decisions as an entrepreneur, if not as a human being.

Everybody has a plan until they get punched in the mouth.

Accurate. His famous quote obviously leans on the ring analogy, but it applies well to your business strategy. Here is the two-part blow-by-blow.

Assume you will fail
Tyson is talking about the hubris behind our strategies. We've got millions of dollars in investment from the top VCs? That doesn't mean you go on cruise control. (If anything, as Mark Cuban says, you've just made the road to success

longer) We raised a ton on Kickstarter? That's just the first step of many - and one misstep could knock us off balance.

The best defense is to assume you will get hit: Critics will drag you, ideas will fail to launch and burnout is real. Your strategy isn't a bulletproof dome protecting you from crisis, but rather a foundation that allows you to keep it together during the inevitable challenges.

Plan to the end
Tyson is explaining that you need to have a strategy deeper than the one in your head, as you are going to get frustrated as soon as you hit a stumbling block. Have you ever prepared for a confrontation by guessing what's going to happen? We're usually way off, as we are skimming over many different chaotic factors like the environment and our opponent's state of mind. Worse, by planning too much ahead of time, we are closing ourselves off to potentially better plans we can come up with based on insights we only see once we get in the proverbial ring.

The best plan is to focus on outcome. How do you want this thing to end? By focusing on the finish line and the important milestones along the way, you give yourself the latitude to get there based on the most practical moves of that dynamic moment. Think about boxing, where a quick hit could swell your eye shut, weaken your arm or literally take your breath away. The ability to pivot quickly without going over the emotional deep end is vital to your success.

There is a reason why every classic strategy book from *The Art of War* to *The 48 Laws of Power* emphasize planning to the end as well as assuming you will not always win. As Tyson knows, the ultimate personal emotional intelligence happens when you accept you don't know what's going to happen next.

15

DOING THEIR BEST

When we undervalue others, we inevitable undervalue ourselves, too

Every entrepreneur learns quickly that creating your own path doesn't make you less reliant on others. In fact, it is the reverse: While a traditional corporate job may hand you one boss, entrepreneurship requires building and maintaining a healthy relationship with co-founders, customers, funders, mentors, and many others.

And the truth is that you won't always like the people you need. Emotional intelligence guru Brené Brown has a quick way to help you get even the most challenging relationship back on track:

The most compassionate people ... assume that other people are doing the best they can. I lived the opposite way: I assumed that people weren't doing their best, so I judged them and constantly fought being disappointed ...

The next time you get frustrated with someone, ask a simple question: Do you believe the person is doing the very best that he or she can?

What often happens is that we realize how much we are judging someone on the basis of our own skills, experience, and strengths. For instance, I have spent decades doing non-traditional work, so I have the discipline to stay focused in unusual work environments such as my home office or in an airplane while traveling. Some people fall apart under the same circumstances, either because they are new to the situation or just have a different personality. Are they doing the best they can, even if the results are poor? In most cases, yes, they are.

Try applying this simple question to the co-worker who always seems to fumble, the family member who regularly disappoints you, or the customer who seems rather dense. As Brown points out in her book *Rising Strong*, the result is empathy-- empathy for the fact that they, too, are doing the best they can with what they've got. It opens up possibilities that you would be closed off to otherwise.

And while becoming a more empathic person is a smart relationship builder, the biggest impact may end up being on you: If you are more accepting of others, then you inevitably become more gentle with yourself.

16
IT ISN'T YOUR MONEY
More resources will just make you more of what you already are now

Podcasts to me, like for millions of people, have become an amazing staple this year. Forget TV: Podcasts are my episodic content. Jenny Blake's *Pivot*, Whitney Johnson's *Disrupt Yourself* and Oprah's *Super Soul Conversations* have transformed my business.

One of the most valuable podcast episodes you can listen to, though, is Basecamp and Ruby on Rails founder David Heinemeier Hansson on *The Tim Ferriss Show*. It is a monster of a conversation, clocking in at 3 and a half hours and touching on everything from smart productivity to brilliant learning strategies to startup mistakes.

The absolute best reason to listen is this gem:

Expectations, not outcomes, govern the happiness of your perceived reality

The line is originally from Heinemeier's own stellar piece about becoming a millionaire in *The Observer*. He and Ferriss spend a significant amount of time breaking down exactly what it means.

Here are three high-level lessons, though you'll want to listen to the whole discussion:

Develop skillsets necessary for after you "make it"
If you are doing 100 hour weeks, sacrificing time with friends and family and not developing any other interests aside from your business, then how do you expect to be happy once you sell your business and suddenly have a life composed of only undeveloped friends and family relationships and withered interests?

Maintain your outside pursuits, however minor the effort. In my own case, selling my first startup didn't land me in early retirement, but it did bring up many emotional issues on how a major part of my life was now gone. Imagine if it had been longer than a year of my life - and imagine if I had sacrificed being a present father, husband and friend along the way.

Your sacrifice now doesn't increase your chances of happiness later
Heinemeier notes that he and Basecamp co-founder Jason Fried manage the wildly successful company on a 40-hour a week schedule. Forty hours! There are administrative assistants that clock in more hours. Heinemeier, Ferriss and even I have met many an entrepreneur that believe sacrificing everything for seven to 10 years means that you'll find success and the ever-elusive happiness at the

end. But there is no guarantee that you'll live to see it, nor that it will actually be there when you get there.

Now is all you've got. If your quality of life sucks now, then, after a decade, you'll be in the habit of burnout, hypertension, depression or any other aliments your body become accustom to. Better to take things day by day and pull in as much enjoyment within the time you have, which is a major premise of Heinemeier and Fried's wonderful title *Rework* as well as this very book.

Focus on process, not success
Success is often a deceptively vague outcome. If your goal is to be rich, then do you have a number in mind, and rich compared to whom, exactly? If your goal is to be famous, then is it to the world, to strangers on the street or to a handful of people who matter to you? And, as I've confessed recently, reaching goals is elusive because ambitious people always move the goal post as soon as they near meeting it.

Focus on the parts of the journey/struggle that motivate you, as they will be the same whether you have financial success or not. Heinemeier says that he enjoys himself the most when nurturing his now-ubiquitous programming language Ruby on Rails or working with his long-time business partner Fried - just like, as he notes, when he was

216

broke living in a tiny Copenhagen apartment. The happiest among us do what we love now because we recognize where we feel the most alive, and, for better or worse, recognize that money won't change that basic principle.

17

YOU ARE ALREADY SUCCESSFUL
You're making more progress than you think

Many of us sit in one of two types of reality-distortion fields. You may think you are more successful than you really are, which means you're in danger of not accomplishing much. Or you may think you aren't doing enough, which means you may burn yourself out because you think you have farther to go.

If you are an ambitious businessperson, then by definition you are the latter. It fuels you. It also can destroy you.

I and long-time author Jeanette Hurt have talked about this for years: We are driven to an incredibly high goal, and just as it is clear we will reach it, we move the flagpole further down the line. Unfortunately, that means never quite being satisfied, nor actually giving oneself credit.

Your insatiable appetite for goal setting may drive you forward, but there's no danger in tempering that trait with some checks and balances. Here's what you can do.

Celebrate every victory

For my latest books, *The Bite-Sized Entrepreneur* and *The Productive Bite-Sized Entrepreneur*, I actually wrote down simple rewards I would give myself at certain sales numbers. I initially had super high markers, but I forced myself to make the victories low. It forced me into the routine of celebrating even minor wins - making the book process even more joyful this time around.

Lean on others

It is essential that you have a small group of people who know your intent and are invested in having you reach your goals. I call them a brain trust, as I've talked about before (Jeanette Hurt is part of mine). When you're not recognizing the success you've made, your brain trust will bring you down to earth and remind you that you did reach your goal - you just decided to move the flag.

Make realistic goals

The further the space between you and your goal, the longer it will feel like you aren't achieving much. Realistic milemarkers not only give you a system to recognize your success, but they also increase the chances of you reaching those momentous goals - since you will have the motivation to complete them from all the minor successes along the way.

18

MIND THE GAP

The space between giant leaps makes the giant leaps happen

Silence often breeds discontent, then enlightenment. I've found that the best thoughts aren't in the hectic speed of the day, the pushing towards bigger ideas or the relentless drive towards superior results. No, the challenge isn't doing the grind for another day – at least for me. The real discipline comes with navigating the space in between, the netherland between doing and not doing, the uncomfortable area that shows no results nor failure.

That uncomfortable space could be when you stop talking about your idea, between the newlywed excitement of a new idea and the actual prototype that you have to share. It can be the time between you launching a rough sketch and you refining the next version, since you have nothing new to show. It could be after your big success and, alas, your next idea is still a sketch on an index card, a document or even just in your brain.

What matters is persevering within that area, that gap, until you make it to the other side. Grinding it out is really easy. So is quitting. But both are smart when done in moderation, but foolish when used as a rule, as either extreme will not get the job done. Instead, it is a matter of breathing in, taking in the vagueness, and accepting that the gap, too, is an equal part of the process.

Sometimes taking a breath isn't a limbo before your next act. Sometimes taking a breath *is* your next act.

MORE FUEL

"You might dread the writing or the running or the leading, but it's the key step on the road to becoming. If it's easier, remind yourself what you're about to be."

-Seth Godin, About to be

1
DO LESS TODAY TO DO MORE
Sometimes the minimum is the best strategy

Giving it 100 percent every entrepreneurial day is an excellent goal, but it isn't realistic. There are days when I easily give 150 percent, while there are others when I struggle to do 80 percent. We talk about always showing up, but rarely address the fact that low energy, decreased time, or scattered focus can make some days better than others. It's just part of being human.

You are sometimes going to have a Minimum Viable Day -- and it is much more fruitful if you actively enter it. Inspired by the Minimum Viable Product approach to shipping enough of a item to satisfy consumers without depleting limited resources, a Minimum Viable Day means doing only the essential work and actively facilitating a slower day with the promise of more productive iterations tomorrow. We talk about products and working with the limited resources we have, but we rarely apply that to our lives.

A Minimum Viable Day should be simple and it should be rare. There are three solid guidelines to actively creating a Minimum Viable Day:

Ship, or it is a day off

Like a Minimum Viable Product, the whole point of a MVD is to "ship" by using the smallest resources necessary. Remember, this isn't a vacation day, nor is it a blank day where you make room for strategic development. I usually set one simple, yet significant goal for the day and use that as the compass for success.

Cut the to-do list in half

Feature creep is real, whether you're talking about adding "must-have" details to your bloated product or squeezing "necessary" meetings into your schedule. Here's a test: If you had a suddenly had a personal crisis or became ill, what items would drop off your calendar in a heartbeat? Take those goals off.

Plan to iterate

Your Minimum Viable Day should help create or build on the foundation of your work, but it absolutely should not be considered the completion of your work. Instead, view it as a basecamp day between long stretches of mountain climbing or as a pit stop through a Grand Prix: It is a necessary pause that will not become the standard for your progress.

A slow day can make us feel guilty, but it is worth putting that aside. By stripping down your day to the essentials, you can differentiate between second-tier priorities and pure fluff. After having a MVD, you may be surprised at how inconsequential certain goals seem in the new light -- and how your productivity goes even higher in the future.

2

THE HOURGLASS PRINCIPLE

Focus on the small and the big will handle itself

The big picture is too much. To paraphrase Tony Robbins, people often overestimate what they'll do in a year, but underestimate what they'll do in five years. The more fully present we can be in the now, the more we can take advantage of any opportunities, and, conversely, slow us down enough to think strategically into the future. Our visions can be mighty, but our milestones should be small, and that is how we can reach our ultimate goals.

The big-picture focus is super common among ambitious people, especially entrepreneurs. It's the founder creating an ad campaign or renting office space when the product hasn't even been finished yet. Systems, as we talked about, are essential to your growth, but you also need to pace yourself so that your most valuable resources, like time and money, are put where they are most needed now.

Rene Rojas, founder of the HubBOG Accelerator in Bogota, Colombia, calls this the hourglass principle. When you first start, focus on the smallest, most doable part of your idea: getting a prototype or early version to your target audience;

talking to an agent or editor about your great book idea; doing a quick-and-dirty website to see if there is interest in your side hustle. It is like sand going through an hourglass. And, like the slow drip, your focus will naturally expand to take in even bigger challenges and ideas. It isn't a matter of running straight into the big picture, but evolving into it based on your feedback, energy, and resources.

3

COMPLETING IS MORE IMPORTANT THAN STARTING

Finishing will give you the energy you're missing today

It's tempting to take nibbles at different activities on your to-do list. If you actually want to be productive, you're better off dropping the multitasking and getting one thing done. In fact, there is a nearly-century old theory that explains why.

The Zeigarnik Effect is named after Russian psychologist Bluma Zeigarnik. In her most famous experiment, she found that waiters were more likely to remember incomplete or unfinished orders than fulfilled ones. It was so extreme that they often could not remember any details of the finished orders.

Her further research supported one simple idea: Completed tasks are rarely remembered, yet incomplete tasks dominate our minds.

The problem is that having several sort-of complete things on your to-do list will make you less productive, as it will require more brain power for you to actually focus. However, if you actually complete the items one-by-one, you are more likely

232

to forget about the finished tasks and give more attention to the important remaining items.

Here are some ways to boost that productivity and fight the Zeigarnik Effect:

Put only one thing on your to-do list
Here's how it works: The night before, decide the one, and only one, thing that must absolutely be done tomorrow. If you're having a hard time figuring out your priority, you can, to paraphrase Warren Buffett, make a list of 10 priorities in order, then eliminate the bottom nine.

The next morning, concentrate on the one thing you have to get done.

For me, the results were spectacular. First, I would almost certainly get the one thing done. Second, it would get done early. Third, it would give me the confidence to go on to the next activity. Fourth, it would bypass all the stress caused by having too long of a to-do list. Lastly, I'd move through each task so fast, I would inevitably get more done than if I focused on the entire list.

Choose a theme for the day
Focus your energy on one particular theme. For instance, you may designate Mondays for correspondence (which, as we talked about in The Bite-Sized Entrepreneur, is a good call!) and

Fridays for planning the following week. This would inform how you schedule your phone calls, so you'd be less likely to get interrupted on, say, a Tuesday when you'd like to do your deeper work since your calls and emails would be designated to the previous day, Monday.

And even if you jump around tasks, you'll still be in the same wheelhouse.

Reward every completion
Give yourself a minute to appreciate a task when it is done. A brief walk, a coffee break, or another simple activity can help you complete whatever is at hand. It also may encourage you to get more stuff done.

The self-imposed reward provides a built-in break, too, which gives your brain the time to recoup and relax, allowing you to focus even better when you need to handle the next task.

4

IS IT REVERSIBLE?
Know the difference between challenging and fatal

Here's what is going to happen when you push yourself: The margins are going to become razor thin. Your emotions will have to expand to new boundaries, your resources will end up being utilized in ways never conceived before, and your management of yourself will have to upgrade to unforeseen heights. "To have more, you simply have to be more," Jim Rohn once put it.

In the process to become more than you currently are, to create a path more extraordinary than average, you'll spend time at the edge of the proverbial cliff looking, if not teetering, towards the drop. It will happen.

And when it does happen, you absolutely have to ask yourself "Is it reversible?" Not "Can it be fixed right now?" or "What can I do to feel less pressure?". The question has to be, "Is what's happening going to be permanent?" Money can be earned again, confidence can be rebuilt, and companies rebirthed from difficult histories.

The panic button is overrated. Your ability to overcome rough patches often isn't based on the toughness of the circumstances, as any unique path *will* be tough – that's why not everyone goes on it! No, your ability to overcome rough patches is usually based on how centered you can remain in the face of chaos. Forget bravery: it's about clarity. It is a scientific fact that the emotional part of your brain will short-circuit your intellectual and creative parts of your brain, the commonly known "Fight or flight" mode where fear and survival drives your decisions. Fight or flight is not strategic, nor is it considering the long-term effects. It renders you incapable of making creative, thoughtful decisions that could not only help you survive, but prosper.

It starts with acknowledging that the work you put in today doesn't go into an empty vacuum. It adds to your momentum and, like a slingshot, all that energy will propel you forward when the moment is right. You just don't know when that moment will be.

Find your treasure
One of my darkest career moments was in 2009. I was fresh home from a self-funded book tour and, based on the five years of work I put into my book *Porn & Pong: How Grand Theft Auto, Tomb Raider and Other Sexy Games Changed Our Culture*, I assumed the offers would roll in from publications eager for me to write for them. I was wrong, and instead I came home to crickets. More significantly, the print

236

industry suddenly fell off a cliff. Stable, century-old publications, magazines that provided my bread-and-butter, were laying off their entire staffs. Long-time editors were contacting *me* asking if I knew of any work. My relatively reasonable San Francisco rent suddenly felt like a ridiculous fortune. I had no money coming in and, with my most reliable editors gone, no prospect of more on the way.

Joseph Campbell called this "the dark night of the soul", when the hero is lost, confused, and seemingly optionless. It is there, too, in this dark night of the soul, that the hero finds a treasure that cannot be gained by any other means. The rest of the hero's journey is spent mastering the newfound treasure and using it to come out of the darkness, bringing the treasure back to the rest of the world like Prometheus returning fire from the gods.

In my case, I heard a strong rumor that Steve Jobs was going to announce a giant iPhone, sort of like a laptop without a keyboard. I talked to a book editor about a simple guide to the device, and the editor loved it. The problem? Internet writers would be covering the gadget as soon as it arrived, and a traditional publisher, at best, would have my book out four to five months *after* the launch. The book would fail.

I then realized there were new options in self-publishing and, after some quick research, learned that digital books were growing much faster than physical books. What if I published my own digital-only book? I rounded up my dad, David Brown, who is an artist, and my colleague Jeanette Hurt, who is a freelance editor, and asked them to help. Sure enough, Jobs announced the iPad in January 2010. It launched April 3rd, and my friends and I stood in line all night to buy one. I spent the following three days exploring every nook and cranny of the device, writing down everything I thought would be useful. *Damon Brown's Simple Guide to the iPad* arrived on digital bookstores exactly a week after the device launch, well before any traditional publishers or even other self-publishers could get their books out. The book went to number one, my rent was comfortably paid into the near future, and I discovered a way to make a living independent of both the capricious print media and traditional publishing industries.

I found my treasure. I wouldn't have been looking for it without the pain. And my previous situation, however dire, became completely reversible.

Develop that muscle
Spirituality teacher Dr. Michael Bernard Beckwith asks this question:

If this experience were to last forever, what quality would have to emerge for me to have peace of mind?

He adds, "I may need some strength or something... name whatever quality. And what happens is your attention starts focusing on that quality rather than resisting the dark night, then the process is sped up. You move through it faster."

Consider that the same thing can happen to you and to me, yet your experience may feel much, much more difficult. It is because I may have a certain learned skill or attitude allowing me to float through the same situation you may consider a crisis. What if the point is for you to learn that skill, too? And, if the situation is reversible, then whatever happens to you may not even do any long-lasting harm.

I have had a few dark years in my career, and without 2009, I wouldn't have developed my voice outside of the traditional publishing industry, which led to several independent books, most recently the very one you're reading right now. I couldn't have known the profound impact my difficult time would have on my career, nor that the financial hardship I experienced would be made up for many times over based on what I was learning. And I didn't have to know.

All I needed to do was ask my favorite question to myself every single day: "Is it reversible?" I'd realize that it was. And, as I realized it, I would feel OK again.

5
RUN PARALLELS
The secret to your success probably isn't where you expect

Entrepreneurs cherish focus. It is what we search for during all-nighters, seek in that third cup of coffee and run after when we pursue extreme goals. But too much focus can kill your productivity.

Here is how less focus can make you even more powerful when you do focus.

Do sprints
Sportsman-turned-entrepreneur Lewis Howes calls it doing sprints, as in focusing on something intensely for a short period, then stopping to reassess. It helps keep your energy and, ironically, help you be more attentive when you do focus. I've been a long advocate, albeit from another angle: Implement palate cleansers between intense work and minimal viable days to give your brain a chance to rest and assimilate information.

Do mindless activities
Greg Mckoewn's *Essentialism* breaks down the process well:

But in fact, we can easily do two things at the same at the same time: wash the dishes and listen to the radio, eat and talk... and so on. What we can't do is concentrate on two things at the same time.

We can use this to our advantage, though: As I explain in *The Bite-Sized Entrepreneur*, our brain actually continues to work on our problems when we stop "thinking" about them. So-called mindless activities gives our mind space to think and create creative solutions. My preferred activity is walking (as it was for Steve Jobs), but it could be going to the gym, cooking and cleaning, or another simple, easily achievable act.

Do parallels
Working on other projects in parallel helps you see things you didn't see before. Consider Archimedes's Eureka moment or Newton's gravity-defining apple while he sat under the tree.

Personally, I gained insights into my last startup, Cuddlr, when I spent time parallel time working on my other startup, So Quotable, just as reading a book on warfare recently helped me understand how to be a more deliberate person.

Everything is connected; everything is useful.

242

6

WHEN IT COSTS TOO MUCH
Sometimes a little investment can protect you from a much bigger cost

Maximizing your time is one of the tenets to success. It is the reason why you hire other people to do things outside of your most productive areas. You can learn a lot by doing the detailed, uncomfortable work, as I talk about in *The Bite-Sized Entrepreneur*, but most often it is like Bill Gates mowing his own lawn: A waste of time, talent and opportunity.

I recently revisited Gay Hendricks' best-seller *The Big Leap: Conquer Your Hidden Fear and Take Life to the Next Level*, and he describes the issue succinctly:

The best way to do things within your zone of incompetence is to avoid doing them altogether.

A colleague of Hendricks spent hours trying to fix his new home office printer. After 13 (yes, thirteen) hours, he finally gave up and hired a neighborhood college kid to set it up. It took him an hour and $100.

How much does Hendricks' colleague get paid for his business? About $1,000 an hour. His colleague wasted the opportunity to make another $13,000. This is the zone of incompetence.

Apply it not just to your career, but your life
Emma Johnson talks about smart delegation in her best-selling book, *The Kickass Single Mom: Be Financially Independent, Discover Your Sexiest Self, and Raise Fabulous, Happy Children.*

Despite watching her money and raising two children alone in New York City, Johnson still swears by outsourcing her housekeeping and her laundry. Why? She knows the financial sacrifice to unload those tasks pales compared to the stress and exhaustion they would cause - and that time, like Hendricks' colleague, could be used to actually make more money.

Cost is not price
Seth Godin once put it extremely well in his piece, "Price vs. Cost":

Price is a simple number. How much money do I need to hand you to get this thing?

Cost is what I had to give up to get this. Cost is how much to feed it, take care of it, maintain it and troubleshoot it. Cost is my lack of focus and my cost of storage. Cost is the externalities, the effluent, the side effects.

244

This is why doing one thing in exchange for another is called "opportunity cost". And it is not just the missed chance to do something else, but the additional energy and effort it may take for you to follow through on your choice.

It is like the frugal consumer driving several extra miles to a distant gas station to save a few pennies per gallon. It feels great to be that thoughtful, but, in the end, it becomes an actual loss. Focus on being practical, not just *feeling* practical.

One big exception
You do not want to skip an experience that will actually make you better at your main competence. For instance, founding, programming, and bootstrapping the app So Quotable taught me a breadth of tough skills, and, without those skills, I'm positive I wouldn't have led my following app, Cuddlr, to success.

More importantly, though, is you should not offload less meaningful activities if they actually help you think through your best ideas. *The Power of Onlyness* author Nilofer Merchant swears by walking (as do I), Arianna Huffington absolutely needs naps and Richard Branson works half days to be his best.

Do not feel guilty if doodling with the new home printer or cutting the proverbial lawn provides space for you to think about your next great strategy. Just make sure you're not wasting your time out of austerity, stubbornness or habit, as it may be more costly than you think.

7

YOU HAVE TO BELIEVE YOU DESERVE IT
You won't make it if you aren't convinced you should have it

When it comes to pop television, VH1's biographical *Behind the Music* was a great way to better understand how to be successful. From rap to rock to Top 40, every group featured went from barely getting by to phenomenal riches and admiration to a seemingly inevitable downfall. And every crash proceeded with some quotable, like "We were loved by the whole world! We couldn't believe our success!"

Foreshadowing at its best.

There are two issues to unpack here. First, the entire world cannot love you, just as, at your very worst, the entire world cannot hate you. Both are an illusion based on your own inner stuff. A good portion of the world is in relative poverty – they're just trying to get their next meal. They are not thinking about your creative success.

Second, if you don't believe in your own success, then it isn't going to last. Consider why million-dollar jackpot lottery winners, on average, end up losing their money within a few years and often end up in massive debt worse off than before. Or why creative overnight successes rarely stay on top after getting into the spotlight.

The key is to actually prepare for your ascension as much as possible. How many lottery winners have an action plan *in case they actually win*? The fact is that they say they want to win, but don't actually believe it. You may want a best-selling novel or a white-hot startup or an amazing financial fortune, but unless you create a sound foundation, you wouldn't know what to do with it or even how to handle it, if you actually got it.

The Big Leap author Gay Hendricks calls this an upper-limit problem: You have the desire for something, but you don't believe you actually deserve the success. It is often built on beliefs we don't even realize are blocking us. For example, if you believe "Money is the root of all evil," and you also say you want to be a millionaire, what is going to happen when you actually get close to your goal? You will likely self-sabotage your potential success, as you don't want to be evil. Or you could change that long-held belief enough so that you allow yourself to succeed. The latter is a little harder, as it requires knowing yourself.

A classic Zen belief is to understand your desire and then to let it go enough so that it can come to you. Passion, patience, and persistence do not guarantee success, but you are guaranteed to not be

248

successful without them. This means that, by focusing on working on yourself, your best life is yet to come. It also means that the best way to get and stay successful is to get out of your own way.

8

KNOW WHO IS AT THE WHEEL
Understand your drive and you'll avoid more accidents

I started speech therapy when I was around four, the same age my eldest son is now. I vaguely remember having a heavy lisp. I clearly remember the emotional frustration of people not understanding what I was trying to say. I began reading when I was around two, but I couldn't communicate well with others until much, much later. The conflict was not easy for me.

By age 21, I had a bachelors and a masters in journalism. By age 31, I had an intense journalism career and six books under my belt. Today, at 41, I've written 21 books in a dozen years and make a living speaking on stages, including at TED.

The ultimate fear? We're talking a year from now, in November 2018, and I'm doing the *exact* same thing I am doing at this very moment. It makes me feel physically ill.

I assume there won't be another time. This is the last moment. The window is closing *fast*. It is time to act! I have to get this out before it is all over. It needs to exist. I have to say it now.

This is my wound.

The wound is that place where you always feel just one step away from fear closing in. It is the place where a seemingly unlimited amount of passion keeps you moving forward. It is the place that drives you. And it will never completely heal.

Spiritual teacher Caroline Myss talks about bringing your wounds to the forefront so you can nurture them and understand them. She says when she helps people, "they can often see how they have lost their energy or power through their overidentification with these wounds or experiences."

At its best, your wound will act like a slingshot: Whatever you think held you back before will give you more momentum than others who aren't fighting the same fight. I just recently noticed the breadcrumbs trailing back to a frustrating early childhood. It is why I must talk to *you*. It is why I do not take it for granted.

Why are you reading this book right now? Why do you need to be something more than you already are now? Find your wound and you'll find your answer – and your ultimate path.

9

BE A GOOD INSTRUMENT

Showing up is the only universal secret to success

Something happens when you think you've got the formula to success: You guarantee that your next effort will be mediocre at best. The cliché term "sophomore jinx" exists for this very reason.

Paulo Coelho, author of *The Alchemist,* one of the most successful books of all time, said this about his masterwork:

Did I write The Alchemist? I'm not sure. I'm sure I was a good instrument... One day, I wrote a book that is, let's be honest, much better than I am. So, one day, you manifest something. This is the real alchemy.

It *is* alchemy. Paulo doesn't know how this stuff works! And neither do I. Whether it is Elizabeth Gilbert personifying genius ideas floating in the air or Steven Pressfield talking about a visiting divine Muse, it is clear that we do not know the source of unique brilliance, excellent timing and, ultimately, phenomenal success.

One thing is clear, though: You can't have a feast on an unprepared slab.

How are you setting the table?

252

10

THE STREISAND EFFECT

Focusing on your weaknesses will only make them worse

Isn't it funny how if you are thinking about something, like having a child or buying a new red car, suddenly you see the desired thing all around you? There is actually a term for it: Baader-Meinhof phenomenon. Your brain is built to pick up patterns, so it will naturally pull out perceived repetition based on your focus.

There is a more popular, if caustic description of this idea: The Streisand Effect. *The Economist*, out of all places, explained it recently:

[Barbra] Streisand inadvertently gave her name to the phenomenon in 2003, when she sued the California Coastal Records Project, which maintains an online photographic archive of almost the entire California coastline, on the grounds that its pictures included shots of her cliffside Malibu mansion, and thus invaded her privacy.

That raised hackles online. The internet's history is steeped in West Coast cyber-libertariansim, and Ms Streisand (herself generally sympathetic to the liberal left) was scorned for what was seen as a frivolous suit that was harmful to freedom of speech. As the links proliferated, thousands of people saw the pictures of Ms Streisand's house—far more than would otherwise ever have bothered to browse through the CCRP's archives. By the time a judge eventually threw the suit out, Ms Streisand's privacy had been far more thoroughly compromised than it would have been had she and her lawyers left the CCRP alone.

And we can totally Streisand our flaws: Focus on your weaknesses and you will see more and more of your flaws in your work and your life. Unfortunately, this will make you more likely to beat yourself up for minor mistakes and you may even emphasize your weak spots to potential coworkers or clients rather than highlighting your capabilities. There is little constructive that can come from blowing up your issues – and there's nothing you can do with the little information gained.

Career strategist Jenny Blake talks about it in her book *Pivot*:

Often the more stuck someone is, the more they tell me what is not working and what they don't want... [and] although it seems like they are clear on some aspects of how to move forward, this information is not all that useful.

It's pretty clear what you don't want to feel. But what do you want to have? To paraphrase another business strategist, Nilofer Merchant, a rebel rallies against something while a leader takes you to a better place. Fussing about your position in life is terribly easy. Clearly expressing where you would rather be takes more effort.

Focus on raw skills
Understand what you bring to the table. A photographer might not know accounting, but she offers the ability to take in both the big idea and the details – a rare ability necessary to either profession. Write down the most basic traits you take for granted. For me, I have spent years explaining complicated, often abstract ideas to the general public, and making it entertaining to boot. How many other ways can that raw skill be valuable? How can it launch me into new directions?

Write down your path
Create an exit plan for your current work, which is an entrance plan to your big goal. The first step or milestone should be relatively small. If you are a public speaker, then the first goal may be someone agreeing to have you speak for free. The next goal may be someone actually asking you to speak. The goal after that could be having your first paid gig.

Make room for greatness
Develop the habits that support your strengths. If you an ambivert (a person who alternates between

introvert and extrovert, like myself), then you can structure your career to support both private time and social time. A so-called weakness may be just the personal system that allows you to function at your highest potential.

Author Louise L. Hay said it well: "Remember, you have been criticizing yourself for years and it hasn't worked. Try approving of yourself and see what happens."

Today is the time to start.

11
YOUR WORK WILL NOT ALWAYS BE
YOUR PAYCHECK
True power comes from knowing who you are
no matter the environment

My real journalism career started in a copy room. I just finished my Master's in Magazine Publishing, lost a job offer the day of graduation and, three months into freelance journalism, became an administrative assistant to make ends meet. When I met someone new in the office, I'd say "Hey, I'm Damon, assistant to so-and-so. And I'm a journalist." Note: This place wasn't a newspaper. It wasn't even remotely connected to media. It was an office downtown. This was two decades ago, so I can't remember specifics, but I do know my new coworkers were looking at me like I was crazy.

One day I was making copies, again, and someone came in to use the tiny station. I introduced myself my usual way. Their eyes lit up: They happened to be in charge of the publishing arm of the company – which I didn't know existed. They wanted to work together. Suddenly, I was really a working freelance journalist.

Here's a hot truth I still remind myself today: How you make your paycheck has nothing to do with how you make your *work*. I don't mean work as in the classic grab the briefcase, "time to make the donuts" way. It is your life's work. It is, as Oprah would say, "work with a capital W".

What's going to happen is that you're going to stretch, and sometimes that stretch means being between the old way you made a living and the new way you are stepping into. There is a gap. Your job is to fill the gap and keep your vision no matter how your money comes in.

I still go through this periodically, as I've moved from newspaper reporter to magazine reporter to published author to blogger to self-publishing author to entrepreneur to consultant to public speaker. Each move to the next level, each move closer to my core intention, is bridged by money and momentum served by my previous identities.

Don't hate the job that gives you funding to fuel your dreams. And don't disavow amazing work you've done in the past, as those raw skills will translate into something you need for your future.

Cuddlr, my app that connected strangers for hugs, succeeded because I knew how to talk to media and, after writing several books on tech and intimacy, I knew what we culturally needed to give users. Would it have gone as big without my years as a journalist? I doubt it, but imagine for a second if I did want to escape my past or not utilize my hard-earned skills in my new role.

258

And an amazing thing happens when you stop worrying about your past: You give the future time to grow. By getting money from stable, if less glamorous areas, then you don't force your Work (capital W) into something it is not. You can focus on understanding your audience, not on making a profit. You can create without fear of repercussions on your daily life. You can experience the joy and, ironically, from that same joy eventually comes income. As I've said in the past, my co-founders and I didn't intend for Cuddlr to be a money maker. For me, I just wanted to move the cultural needle and change how America looked at platonic intimacy. We focused on *that*, and that pure intention led to us making a profit. If we had quit our day jobs and were desperate for money, then the experience for myself, my cofounders, and for the users would have been entirely different, and the success would have been muted, if at all.

Motivational speaker Jim Rohn once said, "If you work on your job, you'll make a living. If you work on yourself, you'll make a fortune." The fortune to be had here isn't just money, though, but the personal fortune of self-knowledge and passion well beyond those living their lives just to get a paycheck.

You don't have to choose. The wisest among us take both the money and the joy.

12

ACT LIKE YOU MEANT IT TO HAPPEN
Unexpected events can become windfalls when you give up resistance

Chances are you didn't expect to be where you are right now. The place you live, the people you spend time with, and the work you do is likely not what you envisioned as, say, a 10-year-old or even as a college-age adult. The randomness of life – or, put more plainly, just *life* – will give you circumstances well beyond your scope of comprehension. Some people believe it is to test you, but it really doesn't matter why. Unpredictable is just what life is.

The best way to strive every day is to actually dive into new circumstances as if they were on your agenda.

Chris Jones, food entrepreneur and co-founder of ChefSteps, explained a similar philosophy his dad handed down to him:

Growing up, my father told me 'Don't worry about what you're going to do' because the job I was going to do hadn't been invented yet… the most interesting jobs are the ones that you make up."

What a breathtaking approach: Uncertainty is your ally. The tools, the skills, and the circumstances you need to make your mark on the world may not even exist yet. You cannot be certain of what's going to happen next. An event that happens in the next 24 hours could change the course of your career and provide a quantum leap in your understanding. It will not be something you can predict, and it will not be something you can control. It will be something that you will have to accept. The less resistance you have to your next adventure, the more you will gain from its arrival.

The philosophical book *The Daily Stoic* refers to this as a "reverse clause", meaning that we make the best out of any event:

If a friend betrays us, our reverse clause is to learn from how this happened and how to forgive this person's mistake... When a technical glitch erases our work, our reverse clause is that we can start fresh and do it better this time. Our progress can be impeded or disrupted, but the mind can always be changed – it retains the power to redirect the path.

It means having faith, religious, scientific, or otherwise, that there is a bigger puzzle at work here. It allows you to show up in the arena, every day, as if it was what you've been preparing for since the beginning of your life. And perhaps you have.

13

YOU ALWAYS HAVE TO COME HOME
Assume you will come back to where you started

Here's what happened the day I was wired the money for the acquisition of my hit app, Cuddlr: Nothing I can remember. Actually, I can remember checking my bank account online at the dining room table and softly saying to my wife in the kitchen, "Well, it's done." Paparazzi wasn't waiting outside, nor was there a big noise coming from my computer. Me and my two co-founders, Charlie Williams and Jeff Kulak, created one of the most popular apps that year, hitting the cover of the *Wall Street Journal* and countless other publications. After my bank notification, I vaguely remember talking about what I was going to make for dinner.

When you get success – and you will get success – the biggest mistake you can make is identifying with your newfound prosperity and assuming that the old you is done.

We've all been in a similar situation: Think about when you dated someone new and became so immersed in the relationship that you stopped calling your friends, family, and other loved ones. The problem, of course, is that the obsessive feeling will be over shortly thereafter, whether you break up with the person or simply began to normalize having this other person in your life.

And what happens after that? You call the people you care about to catch up or, worse, get support after a breakup. The thing is, you haven't maintained those vital parts that helped get you there in the first place. Remember, your loved ones helped make you this wonderful person who was worth dating. They have been busy living their lives and, for that time period, you weren't even keeping a relationship with them.

As I've told my toddler, "I'm glad you feel better, but just because you feel better, that doesn't mean that everything else is OK."

In fact, that may be the most important reason why I wrote this book you're reading right now. The year of my life spent nurturing Cuddlr users, guiding leadership, and putting out fires ended as abruptly as it started. During that same year, good friends got married, close family went through big changes, and my first-born went from baby to toddler. I'm thankful I was there for all of it, but what if I missed these moments in pursuit of the brass ring? The strategies in this series helped me know, in a deep way, my priorities, even as my co-founders and I were the media and late-night talk show darlings, busy fielding business opportunities that we wouldn't have imagined in our wildest dreams. *The Bite-Sized Entrepreneur* ideas made the foundation that helped me stay grounded, remembering, always, that the fame was fleeting and my life, my real life, was continuing independent of any business success I was experiencing. In fact, without my real life, I wouldn't have withstood our 11-month rocket into momentary stardom. It fueled my career, not the other way around.

Your rollercoaster ride will end. Your bestseller will eventually drop off the *New York Times* list, your album will be replaced by another new classic, and your *Forbes* cover will be off the newsstand in a month. You will have to look into the eyes of the people you love and, at worst, justify to yourself that your time in the spotlight was worth sacrificing your connection with them. The trick is that there is no ultimate justification, which becomes clearer as those accolades, no matter how high, inevitably fade into the past.

For each decision you make, remember you will eventually have to come home.

LET'S CONNECT!

This book is just the beginning of your growth. Here's how we keep THE BITE-SIZED ENTREPRENEUR conversation going.

DO THE BITE-SIZED ENTREPRENEUR BOOT CAMP
http://www.bsbootcamp.com

This six-part, self-guided course will bring the best out of your current productivity, focus, and creativity. Taking the book series a step further, THE BITE-SIZED ENTREPRENEUR boot camp is perfect to do at your own pace with my guidance through video, audio, and text. Join through JoinDamon.me to get a special discount on the course and even some one-on-one coaching opportunities!

GET BONUS CONTENT & MORE
http://www.JoinDamon.me

Get your free BITE-SIZED ENTREPRENEUR toolkit to gain even more insight into your next steps. You'll also get exclusive content, early previews of new goodies, and more!

ONE-ON-ONE BITE-SIZED GUIDANCE
http://www.damonbrown.net

I'd love to help you organize your priorities, apply THE BITE-SIZED ENTREPRENEUR method, and make room for your best career. We can set up a time to chat and see if we're a good fit. Reach out at damon@damonbrown.net.

265

SPEAKING AT YOUR EVENT

http://www.damonbrown.net

I am happy to talk about your event and how a discussion on mindfulness, productivity, or entrepreneurship can best fit your needs. International venues are welcome, as are American events, and my platforms include TED, Colombia 4.0 in Bogota, and American University in Washington D.C. My keynote talks are also available and discussed in detail on the next section, **AVAILABLE KEYNOTE TALKS**.

Available Keynote Talks

Damon is available to speak worldwide at select events, conferences, and companies. His audiences have included the main TED Conference, second stage, in British Columbia, American Underground tech incubator in Durham, NC, Colombia 4.0 in Bogota, Colombia, the Adult Entertainment Expo in Las Vegas, and American University in Washington D.C. Damon's talks interweave personal narrative and industry knowledge with actionable strategies. He is also happy to include Q & As and panel discussion as well as moderating panels and interviewing other leaders.

Watch Damon's speakers reel at http://bit.ly/DamonTalks.
Contact Damon at damon@damonbrown.net.

His mainstage keynotes are below:

PROFIT
HOW TO CREATE YOUR TRUE WORTH
Creatives often undervalue their services to the market, to their bank account, and to the world. In this inspiration and practical talk, Damon shares the best ways we can joyfully make a living off our craft, create business partnerships worthy of our skills, and truly be of service to others.

PRODUCTIVITY
THE POWER OF GOOD ENOUGH

What is the number one killer of innovation? Perfection. With perfection, the key motivation often isn't having high standards, but being afraid of making a mistake. In this talk, I share the three powerful strengths you get when you let perfection go.

ENTREPRENEURSHIP
WHY YOU CAN (AND SHOULD) START YOUR SIDE HUSTLE IMMEDIATELY

Believe it or not, we already possess most of the skills we need to create our passion-driven business. So why aren't most people pursuing their potentially profitable ideas? They are intimidated by the small gap in their skill set. In this immediately actionable talk, Damon shares how to easily traverse that gap and explains the three crucial strengths every successful entrepreneur possesses. This talk inspires both potential entrepreneurs and ambitious upstarts.

FIVE MORE GREAT BOOKS TO READ

THE WAR OF ART: BREAK THROUGH THE BLOCKS AND WIN YOUR INNER CREATIVE BATTLES BY STEVEN PRESSFIELD

On the book: What he talks about in the book is something called "Resistance". Resistance is that thing that stops us from spending a little time working on something, the thing that tells us that we're not quite good enough... And the whole book explores how Resistance can be defeated - and how it will never go away.

REWORK BY JASON FRIED & DAVID HEINEMEIER HANSSON

On the book: Before you become successful, use this time to make mistakes without the whole world hearing about them. Keep tweaking. Work out the kinks. Test random ideas. Try new things. No one knows you, so it's no big deal if you mess up.

PIVOT: THE ONLY MOVE THAT MATTERS IS YOUR NEXT ONE BY JENNY BLAKE

On the book: Understand that any confusion or trepidation you feel is normal and, as shown in any of the books, there is already a blueprint to your potential success.

Big Magic: Creative Living Beyond Fear by Elizabeth Gilbert

On the book: Being famous or prolific won't help you succeed again. What matters is the work and your intention. Is your product or service being done with the audience at the forefront? Are you contributing something more to the cultural conversation? Ego-driven enterprises rarely rise as high as purely-motivated work - and we are in the most danger of doing the former after a big win.

The Dip: A Little Book That Teaches You When to Quit (and When to Stick) by Seth Godin

On the book: *If you're making a decision based on how you're feeling at that moment, then you will probably make the wrong decision.* You don't quit when the going gets rough. You quit when you know you've invested more than you'll get out of it. You need clear, measurable metrics to know when to give up on your big idea or business.

Significant Quotes & References

- Table of Contents:
  - Opening quote: Scott Dinsmore, "How to find work you love", from TEDxGoldenGatePark (TED Talks, October 2012)

On Starting
(The Bite-Sized Entrepreneur)

- Opening quote: Steven Pressfield, "The Unlived Life", from *The War of Art* (Black Irish Entertainment, 2012)
- Chapter 1
  - Opening quote: Steven Pressfield, "Resistance is Infallible", from *The War of Art* (Black Irish Entertainment, 2012)
  - Jessica Abel quote: Jessica Abel, "Don't Find Your Passion". Originally published May 26, 2016
  - Adapted from the *Inc.* column "Forget Inspiration. This Beats Passion Every Single Time". Originally published June 16, 2016

- Chapter 2: Lies We Tell
  - Adapted from the *Inc.* columns "Lies Entrepreneurs Tell Themselves" and "Big Lies Entrepreneurs Tell Themselves". Originally published August 15, 2015 and October 19, 2015
- Chapter 3: Effective Procrastination
  - Jessica Hirsche quote: Quoted by Animaux Circus, 2016
  - Adapted from the *Inc.* column "How Procrastination Can Supercharge Your Business". Originally published December 21, 2015
- Chapter 4: Idea Debt
  - Kazu Kibuishi quote: Jessica Abel, "Imagine your future projects holding you back". Originally published January 27, 2016
  - Adapted from the *Inc.* column "Why Your Brilliant Ideas Are Holding You Back". Originally published February 28, 2016
- Chapter 5: Busyness
  - Adapted from the *Inc.* column "3 Awful Reasons Why You Are Obsessed with Being Busy". Originally published April 13, 2016

- Chapter 6: A Good Burnout
  - Adapted from the *Inc.* column "How You Can Turn Burnout To Your Advantage". Originally published October 23, 2015
- Chapter 7: Clutter
  - Damon Brown quote: Damon Brown, "Death by Curation: The problem with recording everything", adapted from *Our Virtual Shadow* (TED Books 2013). Originally published September 2, 2013.
  - Adapted from the *Inc.* column "The 2 Types of Clutter Stalling Your Business". Originally published July 24, 2015
- Chapter 8: Growth Spurt
  - Opening quote: Brene Brown, "Chapter One: The Physics of Vulnerability", from *Rising Strong* (Spiegel & Grau, 2015)
  - Adapted from the *Inc.* column "How to Turn a Growth Spurt Into a Triumph". Originally published March 7, 2016
- Chapter 9: Favors the Prepared
  - Adapted from the *Inc.* column "Why Not Preparing for Success is the Ultimate Failure". Originally published February 26, 2016

- Chapter 16: Martyrdom
  - Adapted from the *Inc.* column "Sacrificing Yourself for Your Business is Silly and Useless". Originally published June 16, 2016
- Chapter 17: Scary Vacations
  - Adapted from the *Inc.* column "Why Entrepreneurs Like Elon Musk Fear Vacations". Originally published October 7, 2015
- Chapter 18: The Smartest Person
  - Adapted from the *Inc.* column "Why You Need a Brain Trust". Originally published September 25, 2015
- Chapter 19: Be Bored
  - Josh Kaufman quote: *Profit Power Pursuit, a Creative Live Podcast, with Tara Gentile*, "Episode 033: Josh Kaufman". Originally aired May 24, 2016
  - Adapted from the *Inc.* column "Why Strategic Boredom Will Boost Your Productivity". Originally published May 31, 2016
- Chapter 20: After the Win
  - Ryan Holiday quote: *The Tim Ferriss Show*, "Useful Lessons from Workaholics Anonymous, Corporate Implosions, and More", Originally aired June 25, 2016

- o Adapted from the *Inc.* column "Why Most People Fail Immediately After a Big Success". Originally published July 7, 2016
- Chapter 21
  - o Steven Pressfield quote: Steven Pressfield, "The Artist's Life", from *The War of Art* (Black Irish Entertainment, 2012)
  - o Adapted from the *Inc.* column "Destroy Average Ideas to Make Brilliant Manure". Originally published March 9, 2016

ON PRODUCTIVITY (THE PRODUCTIVE BITE-SIZED ENTREPRENEUR)

- Opening quote: Mihaly Csikszentmihalyi, "The Roots of Discontent", from *Flow* (Harper & Row, 1990)
- Chapter 1: Create Limitations
  - o Opening quote: Peter Sims, "Failing Quickly to Learn Fast", from *Little Bets* (Simon & Schuster, 2011)
  - o Sleeping quote: *Slumberwise*, "Your Ancestors Didn't Sleep Like You". Originally published May 16, 2013
  - o Maria Popova reference: *Brain Pickings*, "Why Time Slows Down When We're Afraid, Speeds Up as

We Age, and Gets Warped on Vacation". Originally published May 16, 2013

- o Adapted from the *Inc.* columns "Waking Up at 3 Every Morning Made Me Super Productive – Until It Didn't" and "What Having No Time At All Taught Me About Productivity". Originally published July 2, 2015 & July 30, 2015, respectively
- Chapter 2: Know Your Core
  - o Martha Stewart quote: "Ask Yourself, What's the Big Idea?", from *The Martha Rules*. (Rodale, 2005)
- Chapter 3: Death By Networking
  - o Adapted from the *Inc.* column "Why Too Much Networking Will Make You Less Productive". Originally published August 9, 2016
- Chapter 4: Write It Down
  - o Adapted from the *Inc.* columns "The Power of Writing, Not Typing, Your Ideas" and "The Scientific Reason Why You Are Smarter When You Write". Originally published August 7, 2015 & April 28, 2016, respectively

- Chapter 5: Empty Your Schedule
  - Adapted from the *Inc.* column "Why You Need to Add a 'Blank Day' to Your Calendar". Originally published December 18, 2015
- Chapter 7: Walk It Out
  - Adapted from the *Inc.* column "How Walking Can Make You a Better Entrepreneur". Originally published August 31, 2015
- Chapter 8: Stop Measuring Time
  - Pema Chodron quote: "Commitment", *from Comfortable With Uncertainty* (Shambhula, 2003)
- Chapter 9: Do Less With More Impact
  - Opening quote: Steven Pressfield, "The Professional Does Not Wait for Inspiration", from *Turning Pro* (Black Irish Entertainment, 2012)
  - Adapted from the *Inc.* column "Why Being Productive All the Time is a Fool's Errand". Originally published June 16, 2016
- Chapter 11: Alternate Tasks
  - Adapted from the *Inc.* column "How to Boost Your Productivity by Adding 'Palate Cleansers' to Your Day". Originally published November 18, 2015

- Chapter 12: Overextending Yourself
  - Adapted from the *Inc.* column "4 Surefire Ways to Avoid Overextending Yourself". Originally published June 2, 2016
- Chapter 13: Mastering Time
  - Adapted from the *Inc.* column "3 Ultimate Insider Tips from a Time Management Master". Originally published May 31, 2016
- Chapter 14: Put the Coffee Down
  - Adapted from the *Inc.* column "Why 11 am Coffee Makes You More Productive". Originally published September 23, 2015
- Chapter 15: Know Your Prime Time
  - Adapted from the *Inc.* column "Not Productive Enough? Here's a Smart Way to Fix the Problem". Originally published March 14, 2016
- Chapter 17: Opting Out
  - Opening quote: Mihaly Csikszentmihalyi, "Overview", from *Flow* (Harper & Row, 1990)
  - Rembert Brown quote: *Vulture*, "What Andre 3000 Taught Frank Ocean". Originally published August 25, 2016.
- Chapter 18: Looking for a Crisis
  - Steven Pressfield quotes: "Resistance and self-dramatization" and

"Resistance and trouble", both from *The War of Art* (Black Irish Entertainment 2012)

- o Mark Suster quote: *Both Sides of the Table*, "Do You Suffer from the Urgency Addiction? It's More Common Than You Think". Originally published August 18, 2010.
- o Adapted from the *Inc.* column "An Addiction Most Entrepreneurs Have – and How to Manage It". Originally published June 16, 2016
- Chapter 19: Less, Better Email
  - o Adapted from the *Inc.* column "The 1 Powerful Rule That Will Revolutionize Your Email". Originally published May 10, 2016
- Chapter 20: Creating "Me" Time
  - o Adapted from the *Inc.* column "3 Powerful Ways You Can Make 'Me' Time". Originally published January 12, 2016
- Chapter 22: Silence Is Golden
  - o Duke University quote: *Nautilus*, Daniel A. Gross, "This is Your Brain on Silence". Originally published August 21, 2014.

- - Adapted from the *Inc.* column "Want to Boost Your Brain Power? Get Silent". Originally published March 29, 2016
- Chapter 23: Bulletproof
  - Seth Godin quote: *The Tim Ferriss Show*, "Seth Godin on How to Think Small to Go Big". Originally aired August 3, 2016
- Chapter 24: Shadowboxing
  - Pema Chodron quote: "The Empty Boat", *from Comfortable With Uncertainty* (Shambhula, 2003)
  - Srinivas Rao quote: *Creative Warriors Podcast*, "Srini Rao – Be Unmistakable". Originally aired August 30, 2016

ON BALANCE (THE BALANCED BITE-SIZED ENTREPRENEUR)

- Opening quote: Oprah's Super Soul Conversations podcast, "Phil Jackson: The Soul of Success". Originally aired October 9, 2017.

- I: Let Go:
  - Opening quote: Caroline Myss, *Sacred Contracts: Awakening Your Divine Potential* (Harmony 2002)
- Chapter 2: Put Your Mask on First
  - Adapted from the *Inc.* column "How to Stop Burnout with 1 Simple Rule". Originally published September 28, 2016
- Chapter 3: You Need Longer Deadlines
  - Adapted from the *Inc.* column "How Unnecessarily Ambitious Deadlines Can Crush Progress". Originally published October 31, 2016
- Chapter 5: Failure Can Be Success
  - Adapted from the *Inc.* column "How Oprah Conquered Her Biggest Failure (and How You Can, Too". Originally published August 15, 2017
- Chapter 6: Do Good Enough
  - Adapted from the *Inc.* column "Why Good Enough is the Best Path to Serious Success". Originally published February 9, 2017
  - Paulo Coelho quote: Oprah's Super Soul Conversations podcast, "Paulo Coelho, Part 1: What If the Universe Conspired in Your Favor?". Originally aired August 9, 2017.

- Chapter 7: Know Your Sacrifice
  - Adapted from the *Inc.* column "Seth Godin's Secret to Success is Quitting – and So Is Yours". Originally published March 7, 2017
- Chapter 8: The Ultimate Time Limit
  - Adapted from the *Inc.* column "Why Death is the Secret to Your Personal Success". Originally published March 23, 2017
- II: Take In:
  - Opening quote: Bryan Tracy, *How to Start and Succeed in Your Own Business* (Nightingale-Conant 2014)
- Chapter 11: Carry One Thing at a Time
  - Thich Nhat Hanh quote: *The Lion's Roar*, "The Moment is Perfect". Originally published May 1, 2008.
- Chapter 12: Build Like You're Already There
  - Adapted from the *Inc.* column "Tony Robbins' Mentor on How to Build Success Now". Originally published June 8, 2017
- Chapter 13: The 20/20 Technique
  - Adapted from the *Inc.* column "How to Prevent Others from Wasting Your Time". Originally published September 19, 2017

- Chapter 14: Theory is Just That
  - Adapted from the *Inc.* column "The Best Mike Tyson Quote on Emotional Intelligence". Originally published April 11, 2017
- Chapter 15: Doing Their Best
  - Adapted from the *Inc.* column "Brene Brown on the 1 Question You Need to Ask About People You Truly Dislike". Originally published March 16, 2017
- Chapter 16: It Isn't Your Money
  - Adapted from the *Inc.* column "A Millionaire Entrepreneur Shares How to Be Happy (and It's Not by Making Lots of Money)". Originally published December 19, 2016
- Chapter 17: Why You Are More Successful Than You Think
  - Adapted from the *Inc.* column "A Millionaire Entrepreneur Shares How to Be Happy (and It's Not by Making Lots of Money)". Originally published December 5, 2016

MORE FUEL

- Opening quote: Seth Godin, "About to be". Originally published November 29, 2015.

- Chapter 1: Do Less Today to Do More
  - Adapted from the *Inc.* column "Embrace 'Minimum Viable Days' to Boost Your Productivity". Originally published March 18, 2016
- Chapter 3: Completing is More Important than Starting
  - Adapted from the *Inc.* column "This Simple, Classic Theory Will Make You Even More Productive". Originally published July 31, 2017
- Chapter 4: Is it Reversible?
  - Jim Rohn quote: Jim Rohn, *The Art of Exceptional Living* (Nightingale-Conant 2014)
  - Joseph Campbell quote: Joseph Campbell, *The Hero with a Thousand Faces (The Collected Works of Joseph Campbell)*. (New World Library 2008).
  - Dr. Michael Bernard Beckwith quote: Oprah's Super Soul Conversations podcast, "Dr. Michael Bernard Beckwith: Manifest the Life of Your Dreams". Originally aired October 25, 2017.
- Chapter 5: Run Parallels
  - Adapted from the *Inc.* column "How to Not Let Focus Get in the Way of Productivity". Originally published February 28, 2017

- Chapter 6: When It Costs Too Much
  - Adapted from the *Inc.* column "Why Bill Gates Should Never Cut His Own Lawn (and 1 Reason Why He Should)". Originally published September 21, 2017
  - Seth Godin quote: Seth Godin, "Price vs. cost". Originally published October 16, 2017.
- Chapter 7: You Have to Believe You Deserve It
  - Gay Hendricks quote: Gay Hendricks, *The Big Leap*. (HarperOne 2009).
- Chapter 8: Know Who is at the Wheel
  - Caroline Myss quote: Caroline Myss, "Introduction", from *Sacred Contracts: Awakening Your Divine Potential* (Harmony 2002)
- Chapter 9: Be a Good Instrument
  - Paulo Coelho quote: Oprah's Super Soul Conversations podcast, "Paulo Coelho, Part 2: Your Journey to Self-Discovery?". Originally aired August 10, 2017.
- Chapter 10: The Streisand Effect
  - The Baader-Meinhof quote: *Damn Interesting*, "The Baader-Meinhof Phenomenon". Originally published March 22, 2017.

- Streisand Effect quote: *The Economist*, "The Economist Explains". Originally published April 2013.
- Jenny Blake quote: Jenny Blake, "Stage One: Plant", from *Pivot: The Only Move That Matters Is Your Next One* (Portfolio 2017)
- Louise L. Hay quote: Louise L. Hay, *You Can Heal Your Life* (Hay House 1984)
- Chapter 11: Your Work Will Sometimes Not Be Your Paycheck
  - Jim Rohn quote: Jim Rohn, *The Art of Exceptional Living* (Nightingale-Conant 2014)
- Chapter 12: Act Like You Meant It to Happen
  - Chris Young quote: *The Tim Ferris Show*, "#173 Chris Young: Lessons from Geniuses, Billionaires, and Tinkerers". Originally aired July 11, 2016.
  - *The Daily Stoic* quote: Ryan Holiday and Stephen Hanselman, "June 1st: Always Have a Mental 'Reverse Clause'", from *The Daily Stoic: 366 Meditations on Wisdom, Perseverance, and the Art of Living* (Tim Ferriss 2016)

ACKNOWLEDGEMENTS

Writing THE BITE-SIZED ENTREPRENEUR trilogy has been a wonderful, challenging road! There are countless people who have been supportive along the way.

Thanks to the feedback and support from Randy Dotinga, Evelyn Kane, Chia Hwu, Atul Techchandani, Monique Woodard, David Goldenberg, Christina Brodbeck, Mihad Ali, and Mark McGuire, and my editor/goal-buddy/friend Jeanette Hurt and cover artist Bec Loss. Love and respect to my past and present partners, including my Cuddlr co-founder Charlie Williams, as well as my insightful colleagues in the publishing industry, particularly Marilyn Allen and Chris Barsanti. A special blessing to my partnerships that ended poorly; thank you for the lessons.

Articulating the transition from journalist to entrepreneur would have been much more difficult without great sounding boards like E. B. Boyd, Peter Economy, Minda Zetlin, Justin Bariso, Andrea King Collier, Randy Dotinga, A. Raymond Johnson, and Stephan Garnett.

A big hat-tip to Steven Pressfield, Brene Brown, Pema Chodron, Mihaly Csikszentmihalyi, Peter Sims, Mark Suster, Seth Godin, Caroline Myss, Jim

Rohn, Jason Fried, David Heinemeier Hansson, and Alan Weiss. I hope to make even a shred of the significant impact you have made on the many artists, dreamers, and creators.

Love and respect to Kayt Sukel, Jenny Blake, Nilofer Merchant, Srinivas Rao, Laura Vanderkam, Cameron Herold, Kelly K. James, Scott Steinberg, Meagan Francis, Priest Willis, Jeffrey Shaw, Candice Matthews, and Leida Snow. I appreciate your wisdom, camaraderie, and friendship.

Special thanks to *Inc. Magazine*'s Laura Lorber, Douglas Cantor, and Kevin Ryan for supporting the growth of our Sane Success column that inspired this book series. IDG's Jim Malone and Jennifer Dionne, *UNUM*'s Brian Jacob Baker, *Four Seasons Magazine*'s Alicia Miller, Ellis Harman, and Waynette Goodson, *The Costco Connections'* Steve Fisher, and *Entertainment Tonight*'s Shana Krochmal were priceless allies, too.

Lastly, respect to my entrepreneurial parents Bernadette Johnson, David Brown, and Tony Howard, my brother, A. Raymond Johnson, my sisters Deirdra Bishop and Toni Howard, and my wife, Dr. Parul Patel, as well as our precocious boys Alec and Abhi. I love you.

About the Author

Damon Brown is a long-time journalist and author of several books, most notably *Our Virtual Shadow: Why We Are Obsessed with Documenting Our Lives Online* (TED Books 2013) and *Porn & Pong: How Grand Theft Auto, Tomb Raider and Other Sexy Games Changed Our Culture* (Feral House 2008), as well as the coffeetable book *Playboy's Greatest Covers* (Sterling Publishing 2012). THE ULTIMATE BITE-SIZED ENTREPRENEUR is his 21st book and the fourth in the best-selling THE BITE-SIZED ENTREPRENEUR series.

Damon co-founded the social meetup app Cuddlr while being the primary caretaker to his infant son. It went number one on the Apple App store twice, changing the cultural conversation around platonic intimacy. The app was acquired less than a year after it launched, and the whirlwind experience inspired Damon's popular *Inc.com* column Sane Success as well as THE BITE-SIZED ENTREPRENEUR.

You can catch Damon in *Playboy*, *Fast Company*, and *Entrepreneur*, as well as at any locale that serves really spicy food. He lives in Toledo, Ohio, with his wife, two young sons, and bottles of hot sauce.

Connect with him at www.JoinDamon.me or on Twitter at @browndamon.

Made in the USA
Lexington, KY
11 November 2018